KW-247-676

DENIS NEALE

# Halex
# Book of
# Modern
# Table Tennis

WITH A FOREWORD BY
## JOHNNY LEACH
MBE

**WORLD'S WORK LTD**

# ACKNOWLEDGEMENTS

Photographs by Mike Steel
I would like to thank
Mr Charles E. Davies for helping me
with the preparation of this manuscript

Foreword © 1978 by Johnny Leach
Text © 1978 by Denis Neale
All rights reserved

First published in Great Britain 1978 by
World's Work Ltd
The Windmill Press
Kingswood, Tadworth, Surrey

Printed in Great Britain by
Richard Clay (The Chaucer Press) Ltd
Bungay, Suffolk

SBN 437 10600 4

# Contents

# FOREWORD

## by Johnny Leach
### (*World Champion 1949, 1951*)

Players of all ages and standards can gain something of value from Denis Neale's book.

I myself really enjoyed reading it. The contents not only confirm how much knowledge the author has gained in sixteen years of table tennis at the top but establish his ability to pass on this experience to others – a rare gift.

Above all, I find it an inspiring book. It should make you think hard about your preparations, strokes and tactics and also fire you with the ambition to try and follow in the author's footsteps.

I wrote 'try' deliberately because, let's face it, this dedicated, dogged Yorkshireman is a difficult character to follow. Indeed some of his records defy challenge – like his 400-odd appearances for England or his winning of the English singles' title on six separate occasions.

When I first met Denis he was only a schoolboy, he had been selected as a finalist out of some 40,000 young competitors in the annual *News of the World* Table Tennis Coaching Scheme at Butlin's Holiday Centres. The other judges and I thought Denis's game showed a lot of promise and it is always satisfying to see one's hunch rapidly confirmed. Denis became a regular and much valued member of the England team which I had the honour to captain for several years at home and abroad. Then, in more recent years, as Director of the *News of the World* Coaching Scheme, it has been my pleasure to welcome Denis as a highly respected member of our panel of international coaches and judges.

Denis has yet to achieve his ambition to become world champion and on his day he is capable of beating the best player in the world. I can think of no one since Richard Bergmann who can read a game better than Denis and this ability runs right through the book, particularly in his analysis of the methods of ten of the world's best players.

Equally fascinating to most readers will be Denis's detailed accounts of training methods abroad, especially those in the Far East.

Everyone will have his, or her own favourite section but, as I have already written, there is something here of value to everyone. And that does not exclude Denis Neale's fellow stars, none of whom would be too proud to take a tip from a contemporary he admires and respects.

JOHNNY LEACH, M.B.E.

# INTRODUCTION

'My aim in this book is to present as complete a picture of modern table tennis techniques as possible from a top player's point of view.

'The advice is directed at players of all standards, from novices to internationals.

'My hope is to inject at least a degree of professional expertise into everyone's game.'

DENIS NEALE

PREFACE

# 'To Become a Champion'

If you are a beginner with ball sense you will find in this book the guidance to become a skilled table tennis player.

If you are an established player you will find the advice on tactics, and the techniques of world stars, of lasting value.

If you have only a passing interest in table tennis the opportunity is here to gain a deeper insight into the game.

If your ambition is to become a champion, and you possess qualities such as natural flair, will-to-win, and above all dedication to the game, then the professional expertise and know-how contained in these pages will considerably enhance your prospects of success.

But firstly, bearing in mind that all champions were, at one time, absolute beginners, some advice for newcomers to the game.

# CHAPTER ONE

# Advice to Novices

## Age to Begin?

I started to play table tennis at thirteen when by chance I picked up a bat in a youth club. I could equally well have begun to play when I was seven. This applies to all children provided the table isn't too high.

The important thing with young ones is for them to enjoy the game. If they do, their interest is likely to be sustained. Anyone instructing them should remember this. They should not rush things either. Their progress should be gradual remembering all the while that they are growing and having to make adjustments in the way they play.

The age factor in table tennis is very much an individual matter. The test to apply, whether you are seven or seventy, is 'Can I do it?'

This applies equally in championship table tennis where some experts think you are over the hill at twenty-five, and a veteran at thirty.

In this context it is nice to know that some veterans 'can still do it'. I am thirty-two and England champion. Mitsuru Kohno of Japan is thirty, and world champion!

## Play It Naturally

My big tip for youngsters, and beginners of any age, is to play the game naturally. Certain proven principles have to be adhered to – for instance, the spin you have to put on the ball to make it behave in certain ways. Otherwise use coaching hints only as guidelines for your game.

I will be describing how I and other top players produce

11

strokes. Copy them by all means, but if you find you are playing them in a slightly different way, or even in an unorthodox fashion, and achieve control and consistency, carry on doing so and do not worry about it.

In my experience it is not over-coached, robot-like players who become champions, it is those who have mastered the game naturally, often including distinctive and unorthodox strokes in their repertoire.

### The Game
The beauty of table tennis is its basic simplicity. It is this that enables beginners to enjoy the game right from the start. It is easy to score, and the laws governing play are based on common sense.

Full details of how to score, and other fundamental rules, are included in a selection of the laws at the rear of the book. Further information can be obtained from the English Table Tennis Association, 21 Claremont, Hastings, Sussex.

 Become conversant with the laws. If you don't it can result in lost points.

Amazingly this happens even with world class players. Remember the Chinese stars, Kua Yao-Hua and Chang Li, in the world singles finals at the 1977 championships in Birmingham? They both shielded the ball from the umpire when serving and lost points for contravening the laws in this way.

### How to Choose a Bat
When selecting a bat make sure the one you choose feels comfortable in your hand. Select a sponge racket yourself from as big a range as possible. Don't receive it 'blind' as a Christmas present.

The likelihood is that you will be an attacking player in common with most of the top men today. Therefore choose a bat with fast rubbers. I suggest one with 2 mm rubber on each side. This is made easy to do because most bats are sold with an explanatory leaflet.

Later, after experiment and with the benefit of experience, you will be able to assess the merits of various surfaces yourself and become more sophisticated in your choice. To this end I deal in greater depth about sponge rackets in the chapter 'Services and More about Spin'.

Most attacking players use smooth rubber, i.e. with pimples 'in', because it is the most effective way to produce modern topspin. However there are some notable exceptions. The world champion, Mitsuru Kohno of Japan, two top Chinese players, and myself, use pimples 'out'. We do so because we are quick counter-hitters who use little topspin in our flat-hitting games.

If you are a defensive player, and this style of play made a reappearance among a few stars at the 1977 world championships, you need the new long-pimpled rubber on one side of your bat. Without it you will stand little chance against today's spin.

I describe in the chapter 'Services and More about Spin' the most effective way to use this rubber, and why it should be banned!

For details of racket and rubber specifications see the laws at the rear of the book.

### How to Hold a Bat

The two basic grips in table tennis are the self-explanatory 'shake-hands' grip – also known as the 'Western-grip' – and the 'pen-hold' grip which could very well be called the 'chopstick-hold'.

There are many slight variations of these grips, and you

should experiment until you find the hold that gives you reliable control.

Examples of the position of the hand in forehand and backhand strokes appear in the photographs of stroke-play.

**Pressure to Apply**
I favour a firm hold of the bat, but not too tight. The aim is to be able to move your wrist in a controlled manner. So experiment with the pressure you apply until you can do this.

I am often asked, 'Do you alter your grip when changing from forehand to backhand?' The answer is 'yes'. I adjust my index finger slightly. For instance I bring it lower down the blade when backhand hitting. This gives me greater leverage.

**Join a Club**
The way for a beginner to improve quickly is to work hard at practice, if possible against stronger opponents.

One way to do this is to join a club, particularly one with league teams. This should ensure decent playing conditions and reasonable playing standards.

**The Route to the Top**
When you have joined a club your first aim should be to be included in one of the teams. Then as your game progresses you can set your sights on representing your league.

It is important to have targets like this in mind. They provide the incentive to keep practising and playing hard.

**Tournaments**

Any really ambitious player must start entering tournaments early on in their career. It is the only way to gain the experience necessary to get to the top.

Tournaments are held most weekends in various parts of the country. A diary giving full details of a season's events can be obtained from the English Table Tennis Association.

Playing in tournaments is the best way to toughen your game. You do this by:

1. Learning to play against many different styles.
2. Gaining experience in adapting your game to varying conditions.
3. Becoming accustomed to the hustle and bustle and noise that is an integral part of major championships.
4. Learning to adjust your strokes to meet the changes in speed of slow and fast tables.
5. Learning to become flexible in the way you move by playing on different types of floor surfaces.

The experience gained in league matches and tournaments will help you in attaining your next objective – representing your county. To do this you have to do well in trials to which all the best players in the county are invited.


**To Become an International**

By this time you will be a skilled player and no doubt eager to take the next big step – representing your country.

This is an honour you have to earn by winning in tournaments and county matches. In this way you come to the notice of the selectors.

This happened to me when I was nineteen. I made a successful début against Ireland in Dublin, and I can still feel the rosy glow of achievement I felt then.

But becoming an international is leaping ahead in the game, and also in the progress of this book.

So to revert to the beginnings. When you are starting out two questions usually arise. 'What do I wear, and what equipment do I need?', and, 'what is the best way to practice?' These questions are answered in the following chapters on equipment, and stroke-play.

# CHAPTER TWO

## Players' Equipment

Remember, table tennis today is a top international sport, so dress correctly whenever you play. If you look the part of a table tennis player I can assure you it will help you to play like one.

Take pains with your personal equipment. Ensure that your clothing is clean and comfortable. Whenever you play in a tournament have a complete change of gear available. It can be a real morale booster to change from sweaty garments to fresh ones in the later stages of a day's play.

Obtaining the equipment you need should present no problems. The requirements are simple and there is a wide range of well-designed goods to choose from.

Here are the items of equipment I recommend.

1. **Table tennis shoes.** My preference is for light, flexible canvas shoes with a sole that grips well.

2. **Shirts.** I recommend cotton shirts rather than nylon ones because the latter tend to stick unpleasantly to you. Remember rules prohibit the use of light colours in match play.

3. **Shorts.** Ensure that there is freedom of movement with your shorts.

4. **Socks.** Blisters can ruin your chances of winning so take care when choosing socks. Choose, as most top players do, a thick-soled make.

5. **Track-suit.** A track-suit is an essential part of your playing gear because of the importance of keeping warm between matches. Choose one that suits you from the wide range available.

**6. Sundries.** These are some of the extra items I take with me to tournaments: towel and soap, table tennis balls, toothbrush and paste, and a first-aid kit.

I always carry a toothbrush because I find cleaning my teeth, especially just before a final, gives me a psychological lift.

I pack a small first-aid kit because it is handy to be able to stick a plaster on a small cut quickly, or to have an aspirin ready should you need it.

 Any player who has arrived at a match minus his shorts or some other piece of equipment will confirm how frustrating this is. To prevent this happening make use of a check list like the one included here for your convenience.

## CHECK LIST

| | | | |
|---|---|---|---|
| BATS | | | |
| SHIRTS | | | |
| SPORTS SHOES | | | |
| SHORTS | | | |
| TRACK-SUIT | | | |
| SOCKS | | | |
| BALLS | | | |
| TOWEL | | | |
| SOAP | | | |
| TOOTHBRUSH AND PASTE | | | |
| FIRST-AID BOX | | | |
| .............. | | | |
| .............. | | | |
| .............. | | | |
| .............. | | | |
| .............. | | | |
| .............. | | | |

# CHAPTER THREE

# The Shots

When practising the shots described in this chapter keep constantly in mind these key factors – balance, concentration, and the five stages of stroke-making.

**Balance.** When playing your shots, and I cannot over-emphasize this, it is vital to be well-balanced so that your arm and body movements can blend into one smooth action.

Where to position your feet and how to distribute your body-weight to achieve good balance are outlined in the descriptions of strokes.

Don't forget, more errors are made in stroke-play through being off-balance, than for any other reason.

**Concentration.** Cultivate the habit of concentration. Rivet your attention on the ball and your opponent's bat. Note the angle and the direction in which it is moving. This gives you an instant idea of what spin is on the ball and where it is going, and enables you to fully prepare your shot.

To prove I practise what I preach observe my eyes in the photographs of strokes.

 Champions often have time in hand when playing shots even at top speed. Remember, this stems from their ability to concentrate intensely.

**The Five Stages of Stroke Production.** These, used in conjunction with correct footwork and body movements, are:

1. Initial concentration.
2. Preparation for the stroke – with backswing, or by positioning the bat.
3. Moving the bat to make contact with the ball.
4. Follow-through – this aids balance and affects the power of the shot.
5. Recovery, i.e. returning to a well-balanced position to be ready for the next shot.

Now for the strokes, which in this chapter, and throughout the book, are directed at right-handed players. This is to avoid repetition. Left-handers can easily adapt the directions to suit their own style. For a similar reason players are referred to as male.

### Forehand Topspin Drive

Topspin is applied to the ball to make it dip down as it goes over the net and kick-up on contact with the table on your opponent's side.

The ball is made to rotate forwards by striking it with the bat angled slightly forward, and continuing the stroke upwards with a brushing movement.

In the photographs note the position of the feet, bat angle, and follow-through. Also observe how the free arm is used to aid balance.

A smooth transfer of weight from the back foot to the front foot helps to maintain the balance to complete a good shot.

 Because the forehand hit is a longer shot than the backhand hit it is important to get back to the recovery position quickly. Many beginners do not do this and are caught off-balance by their opponent's return.

### Forehand Counter-hit

This shot is used a great deal in modern table tennis because of the speed of the game. It is similar to forehand topspin-hitting but with a flatter trajectory, i.e. hitting 'through' the ball.

With close-to-the-table counter-hitting a short back-swing and compact follow-through is used. At the point of contact the shoulders are square to the net.

Counter-hitting away from the table needs a longer arm movement with a pronounced backswing and follow-through. More body movement is also required with the trunk swivelling from the hips.

Note. Some beginners play a flat forehand by hitting 'inside the ball' to produce sidespin. Virtually no top player employs this method because it does not lend itself to consistency.

### Forehand Loop-topspin Drive

Originally the term 'loop' referred to the trajectory of the ball. Nowadays it refers to the spin on the ball – an exaggerated form of topspin.

Features to study in the pictures are the deep bend of the knees, the position of the bat well below the ball, the long arm action, and the high follow-through.

The stroke is played with a fast brushing action and a rapid follow-through.

An important aspect of the shot is that the body-weight is transferred upwards, almost vertically from the thighs.

Correct timing is of vital importance with this stroke as is the bat angle which varies according to the type of return.

### Sidespin Loop

The sidespin loop is similar to the conventional loop but with the arm action coming around and across the ball.

21

Once again impeccable timing is required and this usually comes only after considerable practice.

**Dummy Loop**

This is a useful variation of the forehand loop shot. It is played with a similar action, except for a slight pause or checking of the bat, just before it makes contact with the ball. This has the effect of appreciably reducing the topspin on the ball.

If your opponent does not spot the adjustment and plays as if for a full loop with a block-shot or chop, the ball will be sent into the net.

As with any clever variation, don't allow your opponent to become accustomed to the dummy or fake loop by over-playing it.

 The aim of the loop-topspin shot is to try and induce high returns to enable you to kill the ball. So strive for consistency.

**Flat Forehand Kill**

The action of this shot is similar to the counter-hit except that the blade angle is more forward.

The shot is faster than the counter-hit and this speed is achieved with a whip-like wrist action and follow-through.

Body-weight in this instance is transferred from right to left with a vigorous swivel movement from the hips.

 Use this shot as much as possible – it is the best way of winning points.

**Scissors-kick Kill**

This shot is a speciality of mine. I use it to deal with balls that bounce high from lobbed returns. The technique is to leap into the air, execute a scissors kick, and kill the ball at the top of its bounce. It is in effect a flat-kill in mid-air.

It is not an easy stroke to perfect because precise timing and a certain gymnastic agility are required, but because of its spectacular effectiveness, and audience appeal, it is well worth the effort to do so.

### Backhand Counter-hit
Note that with this stroke the ball is taken in front of the body. It is also taken earlier than the forehand, often on the half-volley.

The stroke is short throughout, and a controlled wrist action is used.

Generally a good balance is maintained with legs apart and the right leg just in front of the left. An exception to this is when playing against short balls, then the right leg is pushed further forward.

 Most players have a weakness with this backhand shot simply because they do not practice it as much as their forehand. Don't let it happen to you!

### Backhand Topspin Hit
The basic movements for a backhand topspin shot are the same as for the backhand counter-hit. The difference is that instead of hitting 'through' the ball, you lift it with an upwards brushing motion of the bat to impart topspin.

### Backhand Loop-topspin
This stroke starts with the bat below the table. The knees are bent and, as with the forehand loop, body-weight is transferred upwards from the thighs. It is played with a rapid wrist action – the bat brushing the ball and following

through in a straight upwards direction. It is usually employed against a chopped ball.

 This is the newest, and certainly one of the most difficult shots to learn. It has only been mastered by a few world stars – so do not be disheartened if you have problems with it.

**Backhand and Forehand Block-shots**
The backhand block-shot is usually taken on the half-volley over the table.

As with the backhand counter-hit the body should be positioned behind the bat.

Body-weight is supported on the right leg on contact with the ball.

Good control depends on precise timing, a sensitive touch, and the bat being angled correctly in relation to the spin on the ball.

Against slower balls a faster follow-through is needed.

In today's game this shot is often used to smother top-spin.

Points can be won by varying your bat angles cleverly to catch your opponent out of position.

 Time spent in practising this shot is worth-while because of its effectiveness against the modern loop game.

Because of the speed in modern table tennis I do not recommend the forehand block-shot. It requires a difficult wrist movement, and angled shots are not easy to play. This tends to create openings for your opponent.

**Push Shots – Forehand and Backhand**
It is vital in today's game to master the forehand and backhand push strokes. Not so much the old-fashioned

long pushes employed purely to keep the ball in play, but light, short, touch-shots. These are used particularly to return short services equally close to the net in order to prevent the server from dominating the game.

When playing push strokes it is important to position your feet so that you have a solid base for the shots. Lead in with either left or right leg, depending where the ball is placed. Knees should be bent, waist loose, and your body-weight transferred to the front leg as you make contact with the ball.

In the photographs of both forehand and backhand pushes, note the straight forearm action at the moment of contact. At this point the bat is always underneath the ball, but the bat angle varies in relation to the spin on it.

## Drop-shot

This is a delicate shot similar to the push stroke, but only to be used when your opponent is well away from the table.

Very little follow-through is used, and the aim is to 'drop' the ball just over the net so that your opponent is either unable to reach it or has difficulty in doing so.

Being a touch shot it needs a lot of practice to get it right, particularly to eliminate the danger of setting up the ball for easy kills.

The shot can be used in an attempt to tire your opponent by forcing him in and out from the table.

## Defence

Although in recent years very few top men players have used chop defensive strokes as an integral part of their game, in the 1977 world championships three world-class players did so. They were Huang Liang and Liang Ke-Liang of China, and Norio Takashima of Japan.

The two Chinese players proved to be potently effective

by using a new style long-pimpled rubber on one side of the bat. As I mentioned earlier, this is discussed fully in the chapter 'Services and More about Spin'.

## Backspin

The action of chopping, or under-cutting the ball, causes the ball to rotate backwards in flight. In other words you are imparting backspin.

On a fast table this causes the ball to keep low, sometimes even skidding through.

On slow tables, however, the ball slows on making contact with the table on your opponent's side and tends almost to 'hang' in the air.

## Forehand Chop

The starting-point of this stroke is just below shoulder height and to the side of the body.

The bat, which is angled backwards, is brought down in a slicing action. At the point of contact it is under the ball. Complete the shot with a smooth follow-through.

When playing a forehand chop, knees should be bent and body-weight moved downwards and forwards.

## Backhand Chop

With the backhand chop the starting-point is slightly lower than with the forehand. It is mid-way between the waist and shoulder.

Bat angle, point of contact, follow-through, and body movement are similar to those of the forehand stroke.

## The Float

The float is a stroke played with a simulated chopping action. It looks as though you are imparting backspin, but a lightness of touch puts little spin on the ball.

If an opponent doesn't 'read' the shot correctly he will

lift as for backspin and return the ball high, or off the end
of the table.

 One way of improving your defensive play
dramatically would be to obtain sheets of the
new long-pimpled rubber as used by some
Chinese players on one side of the bat.

**Topspin Lob Defence**
'Lobbing' is a defensive method used mainly by attacking
players when forced out of position away from the table.

The ball is 'lobbed' high with varying amounts of spin
on it. Every attempt is made to play the ball deep to make
it difficult for opponents to return. Lots of practice is
needed to develop this skill.

Jacques Secretin, France's left-handed European champion, is the supreme exponent of this eye-catching technique.

**Timing**
I have referred to timing in the descriptions of various
strokes. But what is timing?

Timing is the precise moment at which the bat makes
contact with the ball.

Co-ordination, balance, technique, concentration – all
combine to achieve correct timing. But essentially good
timing is when you produce a flawless table tennis stroke.

Correct timing varies from player to player because of
physical differences. It is usually the product of long hours
of practice and experiment. You know you have it when
your strokes are flowing with a natural rhythm.

# CHAPTER FOUR

# Champions' Unorthodox Shots

I mentioned in the chapter 'Advice to Novices', that champions sometimes play in unorthodox ways. Here are some striking examples of the way they do so:

Danny Seemiller, the left-handed U.S.A. star, plays his backhand in an unorthodox but highly effective way. His technique is to turn his wrist over so that he is producing a backhand stroke with the bat in the forehand position.

His younger brother, Rick, who is right-handed and also represents the U.S.A., plays his backhand in the same fashion.

The bewildered looks on some of their opponents' faces testify that the shot works.

I have a built-in unorthodoxy in my forehand drive which causes the ball to swerve.

When I was seven I broke my right arm in four places. The bones failed to set properly and consequently my arm movement is slightly out of the ordinary. It is this that helps to produce my unorthodox, but point-winning, forehand hit.

Huang Liang, the Chinese ace, uses a jab-block shot that baffles world stars, and wins points against them. This is a stroke which Huang certainly did not learn from a text-book or a coach.

Istvan Jonyer, of Hungary, the former world champion, uses a bat with an extended handle. He grips it low down to obtain the extra leverage necessary to play his wonderful loop shots. Unorthodox, but devastatingly effective.

World champion, Mitsuru Kohno's ready position for

doubles matches is remarkable. He stands four to five yards behind his partner and comes running in to play his shot like a sprinter leaving the starting blocks. It is his way, and it works.

So do all the shots mentioned here even though they may send shivers up and down the spines of most table tennis coaches. They are played with control and consistency, and as I underlined earlier, this is the test to apply to any similar shot.

# CHAPTER FIVE

# Playing Drills

Once you have learned how to play individual shots you will realize that this is only part of the battle.

The next stage is to be able to blend them together to form an effective game.

The best way to do this is with organized practice, and a lot of it.

If you can enlist the aid of an understanding partner, and obtain a plentiful supply of balls, you are off to a good start.

Map out a programme of exercises and take it in turns with your partner to be the 'controller' or 'feeder'.

Be methodical, and with each exercise have a definite purpose in mind.

It may be that you or your partner are not skilled enough to control the exercises with your bat. This presents no problem. With most routines it is perfectly in order for the controller to throw the ball to the desired spot on the table. This is where a good supply of balls comes in.

It is of supreme importance to remember that how you practice vitally affects your game. The shots and movements you repeat ten thousand times and more in practice become, in the end, 'your game'.

The aim is to get it right as soon as you can and to keep on getting it right. So analyse your strokes and movements constantly, especially any errors you make.

If in difficulties check closely with the advice I give in this book. Additionally discuss any problems with more experienced players. It is often so much easier for someone looking on to spot what is wrong than for you to come up with the answer yourself.

Any bad habits you pick up by faulty repetition in training will soon be exposed where it counts – in matches. Equally your good moves will also show where it matters – in winning games.

### Drills

The following drills are based on those used at international training camps.

With a little imagination they can be adapted and extended to cover most of the shots you need to practice.

The time you devote to each one is a matter of personal preference but I suggest fifteen minutes.

**Drill 1.** Here is an exercise for short push strokes. A club mate acts as controller and serves continuously short services. You try with short forehand and backhand pushes to knock over a series of match-boxes placed close to, and parallel to the net on his side.
(See diagrams for the following exercises.)

**Drill 2.** This exercise is particularly good for improving side-to-side footwork, and forehand hitting from different positions. It can also be used for any of the forehand strokes.

(1) The controller directs the ball to points 1, 2, 3 and 4, then to 4, 3, 2 and 1.

(2) The receiver hits the ball in the direction from which it came and then moves to the next point.

**Drill 3.** Practising moving forwards and backwards is important. Here is an ideal routine for this.

The controller plays the ball short (1 and 3) and long (2 and 4). The receiver moves alternately forwards (1 and 3) and backwards (2 and 4).

A similar sequence of balls can be played to the backhand side of the table.

**Drill 4.** This drill is designed for practice in playing short and deep shots. It is also useful in providing practice at avoiding the shaded section of the table. This is the area of the table from which it is easiest for an opponent to kill balls.

Vary the exercise by playing your shots from different positions.

The routine is also an excellent one for service practice.

**Drill 5.** Here is an excellent exercise for speeding up footwork and developing alternate forehand and backhand hitting.

Start with a fast forehand service diagonally to the controller. He hits this straight down the line to your backhand. This is countered with a backhand hit diagonally to the controller's backhand. Once again he hits down the line – this time to the receiver's forehand. Repeat the pattern.

Note, the expression 'down the line' means playing a ball parallel and close to the 'sideline', i.e. the 2 cm broad white line at the edge of the table.

# DRILL 2

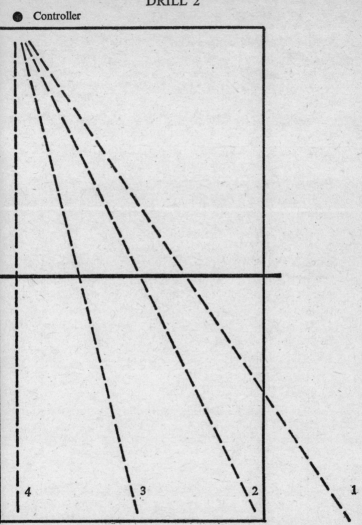

● Controller

4    3    2    1

Yourself ●

# DRILL 3

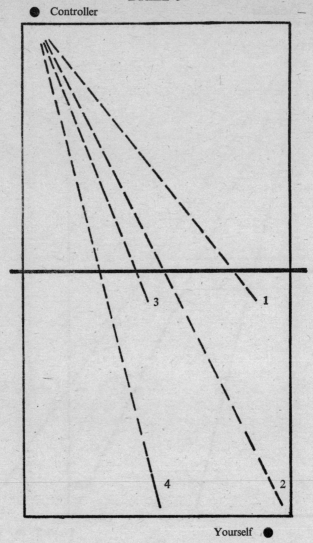

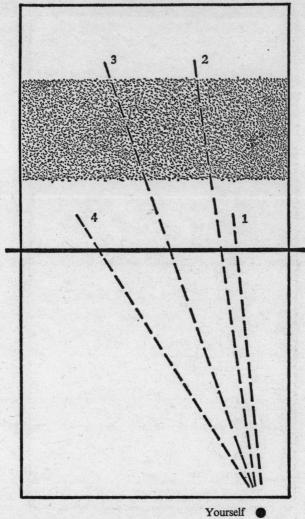

Yourself ●

# DRILL 5

Controller

Yourself

36

# CHAPTER SIX

# Services and more about Spin

## Services

Services and the return of service have become the most important features of modern table tennis.

Evidence of this was provided at the 1977 world championships in Birmingham where even world stars lost points directly against Chinese services.

The Chinese aces achieve their serving skill by practising hour after hour.

 One exercise they use for side-spin services is to place a basket at the far side of the table. They have to keep serving until they fill it with two hundred balls. Only when this is done can they move on to other training activities.

Any player who is willing to devote similar time and effort to improving their serving will do so by at least one hundred per cent.

## Ways to Improve Services

Remember when you are serving it is the only time during the game when your opponent has no influence on the game. He cannot rush you or put you under pressure. You can just take your time.

You should aim to learn a wide variety of services. Do this by directing the ball to different parts of the table. Change the speed, and spins on the ball.

37

A flexible wrist movement is needed for all services.

Try to keep your opponent guessing with clever variations. Two services I find particularly effective in this are:

(a) Short services, with varying spins, to the forehand – this tends to bring the opponent right into the table and often out of position for my follow-up shot.
(b) With a similar action I serve a rocket-like topspin serve to my opponent's backhand.

### High-thrown Service
A recent development in serving is the high-thrown ball. This enables the server to put more spin on the ball because it is travelling faster than with lower services. I refer again to this service in the chapter 'My View of the 1977 World Championships'.

### Recovery
Another point well worth emphasizing is that after serving, as with any other stroke, a quick return to the recovery position is essential.

### The Ready Position
The ready position is the position you take up when waiting to receive service.

As you can see from the photograph it is an alert posture, with legs apart, knees bent, and the body leaning slightly forward.

Where you stand depends on the game you play. If you are a two-wing attacker a central position eighteen inches from the table could be ideal. If you are predominantly a forehand hitter the tendency will be to take up a position on the backhand side. Many of the world's leading players do so, particularly pen-hold hitters.

 If you are not completely ready to receive service hold your free hand up in the air to indicate the fact to your opponent and to the umpire. This is standard international practice.

### How to Return Services

Important points to remember when returning service are:
1. Relax, but concentrate one hundred per cent.
2. Watch your opponent's bat action to see what spin is on the ball.
3. If experiencing difficulty with spin services, play the ball as late as possible. The later you take it the less spin there is on it.
4. Aim to be well-balanced at all times.

### Short Services

Two ways of returning very short services are:
1. With a delicate push shot from a well-balanced position.
2. Using a forehand flip shot. This is a short, 'wristy' stroke which imparts a degree of topspin.

As the name indicates you have to flip the bat over the ball, and with fast rubbers speedy returns can be produced.

You also have to reach well forward over the table to play the shot in much the same way as you do for the push.

### Eye on the Ball

One exception to keeping your eye on the ball occurs when the server throws it high in the air. Do not follow the ball up. You may be dazzled by lights, or lose the ball in the background. Just watch your opponent's bat action at the point of contact.

 Stellan Bengtsson, Sweden's former world champion, prepares to deal with the difficult Chinese services in an unusual but most effective way. He 'reads' the spin by watching the print on the ball and the direction in which it is spinning off the table.

## More about Spin

There are basically three spins in table tennis – topspin, and backspin, which are dealt with in the chapter on stroke play, and sidespin.

Variations of these spins are achieved by changes of speed.

Sidespin is produced by directing the bat around the ball in a brushing motion. This causes the ball to spin left or right.

Once you have learned how to produce spins it is then vital to be able to 'read' the spin your opponent puts on the ball.

You do this by watching the angle of his bat and the direction in which it is travelling.

Generally the ball will spin in the direction the bat is moving.

I say generally because of the new long-pimpled rubber which makes a nonsense of this.

It is used, as I have said, by top Chinese players on one side of the bat. On the other side they have a different rubber.

When the long-pimpled side is used with a backspin action, instead of applying backspin it puts no spin on the ball at all!

Thus, with the Chinese switching sides at random

during the rally, you never know for certain what is on the ball. You are guessing most of the time.

It means you are playing against your opponent's equipment rather than his skill.


## More about Sponge Bats

Why a sponge racket? Well no top player today uses the old-fashioned 'hard rubber' bats. They use a sponge bat because of the effect sponge has on the ball.

This is what happens. The layer of high-density sponge between the rubber and the wood has a springboard effect. The ball is absorbed by the rubber and sponge and there is a propelling effect as the ball rebounds. With hard bats you do not get this help.

If the rubber is 'reversed', i.e. smooth, it retains contact with the ball for a fraction of a second longer than if it has 'pimples out'. It is this split-second extra contact time that enables a player to impart a greater amount of spin with his smooth-covered bat.

With 'pimples' the amount of surface area effectively in contact with the ball is less and accordingly so is the amount of spin that can be put on the ball.


## Which Sponge Bat?

Players and manufacturers are constantly seeking ways to improve performance or to gain some advantage by means of new bats or new rubbers.

This accounts for the ever-increasing variety of bats on the market.

A recent addition is a black, sticky-type rubber designed to produce extra spin by 'gripping' the ball more.

Then there is the further complication of a wide choice of wood, from one-ply through to nine-ply.

This multiplicity of choice makes it difficult for many

players to decide which bat to adopt. But a decision has to be made. Do it this way:

1. Follow the common sense advice given in the chapter 'Advice to Novices'.

2. Try out as many different bats as possible.

3. Find out the type of racket used by the top player whose style most closely resembles your own, and try that.

4. Finally, remember however wonderful a bat is said to be, in the end it is your skill, and the ability to use it that counts.

 At all times ensure that your bat rubber is clean and resilient. Apply this test. Draw a ball lightly over the surface. If the ball fails to grip and slides easily over the rubber, the rubber either needs replacing or cleaning. This can be done with lukewarm water.

# CHAPTER SEVEN

# Winning Tactics

Every game of table tennis between players of equal ability can be won by superior tactics.

It would seem vital therefore to gain as wide a knowledge of tactics as you can. But, in my experience, this is one area of the game in which most players, including some internationals, are lacking.

This chapter presents any player in this category with the opportunity to rectify the situation.

## Pre-match Opportunity

A tactical appreciation of your opponent, if you haven't met previously, begins before a game in the pre-match knock-up. Use this time to assess your opponent's strengths and weaknesses. Many players throw away a valuable opportunity to do so by knocking-up aimlessly.

## Tactics Against a World Champion

An example of how useful this can be, even at the highest level, occurred in the 1973 world championships in Sarejevo, Yugoslavia.

In the first round I was drawn against the former world champion, and No. 1 seed, N. Hasegawa of Japan. I had played him previously but had not discovered a weakness. In the knock-up I experimented by playing soft, short-balls to his backhand. I noticed he appeared tentative when returning these.

This knowledge proved a decisive factor when, after a

tense, fluctuating battle we reached 10-all in the fifth set. It was then I began to use the short-ball tactics.

Incredibly I won six quick points, and with such a boost to my confidence I was able to run out a comfortable winner.

## Styles

Basically table tennis tactics are methods of play designed to win points in particular situations.

These methods obviously vary according to the style of play of your opponent.

There are many individual styles but they can be grouped into three broad categories – quick-hitters, loop-spin exponents, and defensive players.

Equally, depending on your game, there are general guidelines you have to follow when deciding on the tactics to adopt against a particular style.

Here then are descriptions of the tactics to be used against a wide range of styles. They have been tried, tested, and proved under the most exacting conditions, and where it matters most – by myself in the championship arena when beating many of the world's stars.

## Tactics to be used by:
## Quick-hitters against Loopers

The prime object for a quick-hitter is to stop the looper getting in with his big spins. This can be done by playing short and long balls to bring him close to the table and then force him back. Changes in pace add to the effectiveness of this tactic.

These moves combine to spoil the looper's rhythm and to reduce the amount of spin he is able to put on the ball. When this happens the hitter has the opportunity to kill the ball past him.

44

I have used these tactics successfully against former world champion, Istvan Jonyer of Hungary.

### Quick-hitters against Defensive Players
Remember most defensive players don't win the point. You lose it! Therefore be prepared to work and work and be patient, particularly against skilled, dogged, determined players.

Changes of pace and direction are important. Try to move your opponent from side to side, and in and out. The object of this is to induce a loose return for you to kill.

### Quick-hitters against Quick-hitters
This is the counter-hitting game which at its best provides the spectacle crowds love to watch.

With close-to-the-table exchanges one player often begins to get on top, out-speeding and out-angling the other. To counter this the slower player should step back a couple of paces. This gives him more time to play his shots and cover the angles.

On occasions I have been outsped by my England team colleague, Des Douglas, and have adopted these tactics. I did so successfully when winning the 1977 Norwich Union English Closed Championships.

When an opponent steps back against me I counter the move by slowing the pace to bring him close to the table again.

### Loopers against Quick-hitters
A looper aims to get his big spin in directly from return of service against a quick-hitter.

This is known as the third-ball attack sequence and was widely used in the 1977 world championships. It is service, return of service, followed by an aggressive shot.

To do this a looper must develop good services.

When a loop-topspin player is unable to play his big loop early against a quick-hitter he endeavours to close the game up.

Dragutin Surbek, of Yugoslavia, the former European champion, did so against me by pushing the ball very short to bring me in close to the net, and then pushing deep. This stopped me hitting and enabled him to loop again.


## Loopers against Defensive Players

If a looper plays a defensive player of equal standard the looper should always win. This is due to the spin and speed which comes from modern bat surfaces.

A looper's tactics against a defender are much the same as those of a quick-hitter, i.e. variations of pace and direction, and patience.

The big difference is the looper's spin which is aimed at producing high returns for quick kills.

Every opportunity to kill the ball should be taken. Continuous looping only serves to play the defender in, and the looper ends up making the mistakes.


## Loopers against Loopers

This is the technique of the Seventies, and because flawless timing is a vital part of it, it is the most difficult game to play.

Generally the winner of a point in exchanges between loopers is the one who gets in first with his big spin and drives his opponent back from the table. He can then dictate play from his close-to-the-table position.

If neither player gains the ascendancy in this way it is the most consistent player who will win. Such consistency can only be reached by years of dedicated practice.

This style of play is a Hungarian speciality and Tibor Klampar, Gabor Gergely and Istvan Jonyer are the world's top exponents of it. They use their serving skills to take the initiative and then loop from either wing.

## Defence against Quick-hitters and Loopers

Today it is impossible at the top men's level to win with a totally defensive game unless you use the recently developed long-pimpled rubber. (This is discussed fully in the chapter 'Services and More About Spin'.)

I know of only two world-class defenders among the men, who do not use the new long pimples. They are Norio Takashima of Japan, and Christian Martin of France, and both of them hit well on either wing.

My recommendation is, 'Don't attempt to play a totally defensive game unless you use the new rubber.'

Only by doing so can the traditional defender's methods of mixing heavy and light chops with 'float' returns hope to prevail.

## Defence against Defence

When two out-and-out defenders meet it often results in a long, drawn-out game. It is in these circumstances that the expedite rule is introduced. (A full explanation of this is given in the laws of the game at the rear of the book.)

When this happens the player who possesses the more effective hit will usually win.

The defender with an indifferent attack should tempt his opponent into hitting and hopefully making mistakes before expedite is introduced at the end of fifteen minutes.

Conversely the defender with a reliable hit should keep the game tight and play for expedite in order to capitalize on his superior hitting strength.

Defenders should work at the techniques of expedite play in practice so they are not caught unprepared when they meet it in match play situations.

### Left-handers

The golden rule to follow with left-handers is to put in plenty of practice time against them. This gives you experience against their awkward angles, and practice at neutralizing their usually strong forehands by playing to their backhand wing.

### Tall and Short Players

A good general rule of tactics to remember is: against tall opponents play the ball to their body; against short players play wide-angled balls to take advantage of their lack of reach.

### Self-control

Don't give your opponent a free bonus by showing him you are upset, or by generally losing your cool.

### Captaincy

At times when you are struggling in a game and are unsure where you are going wrong tactically – and this happens with the best players – a knowledgeable team captain can come to the rescue with a few words of sound advice.

It is in such circumstances that a captain proves his worth.

But, what is a good captain?

In my opinion he should have the following qualities:

1. Players must respect him.
2. They should be able to believe in him.
3. It is essential for him to have a comprehensive knowledge of table tennis.
4. In order to give tactical advice he must know the capabilities of his players.
5. He must know, or have an instinctive feeling for, the kinds of pressures his players are likely to face.

6. He should have the ability to inspire confidence in a team.

Captains with all these attributes are rare but one man who possesses them in full measure is Johnny Leach, twice world single's champion, and a former England team captain.

His forte was inspiring confidence in his team. He could send you back into the arena after a first game mauling, so full of heart that you emerged a winner from a seemingly impossible situation. He was a magician in this respect.

**Analyse Your Performance**

 An excellent way to improve your tactical know-how is to analyse both your wins and losses.

I do this constantly because it pays dividends. For example, a week before the 1977 Norwich Union English Closed Championships I lost to English international Andy Barden, 21–9, 21–9, in the Cleveland Open. I examined this loss thoroughly, came up with the correct answers and in the 'English' I beat him 3–0.

Finally, I cannot emphasize enough how important it is to think on your feet in match play. Try to discipline yourself to do this at all times.

# CHAPTER EIGHT

# The Cheating Side of Gamesmanship

When you have been around the table tennis circuit a while, you come to realize there is an aspect of the game rarely touched on by coaching manuals. It is gamesmanship.

Whether you consider the dodges, manoeuvres, 'psyching', and various ploys that constitute gamesmanship to be ethical or not, it is as well to know about them. If you don't your game will be thrown out of its stride when you meet up with these tricks of the table tennis trade.

And meet up with them you surely will, for many players indulge in at least some of a whole range of questionable tactics from time to time.

Some, including a number of leading continental players, are honours graduates in the art. They pull out all the stops to unsettle you, and to win points by whatever means they have to hand.

If there is a weak umpire they will foul serve.

If they know an opponent is susceptible to abuse they will snarl insults across the net.

When the game isn't going right for them they will return a 'dead' ball to you, not by throwing it in the normal way, but by rolling it along the floor, making you stoop to pick it up.

Nastiness is the name of their game and you have to steel yourself not to be upset by their antics.

Not all gamesmanship comes into this category however. There are some moves I consider to be legitimate.

Slowing down the game at psychological moments is

one. For instance if you reach a critical 19-all situation in the deciding set, this is the time to try to break your opponent's concentration. Do this if you are serving, by delaying your service. If you are receiving, hold up the game by towelling down.

Talking to your opponent before the game is also above board. Tell him how well you are playing. Express the hope that he may do better on some future occasion. This 'psyching' works, as many of my beaten opponents can testify.

If you are playing with a ball you find unsuitable, break it, but make it look like an accident. This is fair because your concentration will suffer if you don't, and you will be handing your opponent an advantage he does not deserve.

Other dodges though are simply cheating. Here are some of them:

1. The Sweat Trick. This is where unscrupulous players wet the ball with spit or sweat just before they serve. When you play the ball it either plonks lamely into the net, or swerves away out of control.

Be on the lookout for this and if you spot it happening inform the umpire immediately. Once a point has been lost it cannot be re-played.

2. 'Sorry' Merchants. Be watchful for tricky opponents who try to influence the umpire's call by saying 'Sorry', when their shot just misses the table. Some officials may be fooled into thinking the ball has touched and award the point to the trickster.

3. Ball Switching. When playing in tournaments be sure that the ball you start the game with is the one you continue to use. Some twisters change the official tournament ball for a different brand more suitable to them.

These then are some of the more doubtful practices to be found in table tennis.

You have to decide what is, or is not, acceptable, and act accordingly.

My advice, from long experience, is that there is only one way – 'play hard and play fair, but do not stand for any chicanery from the sharp operators'.

# CHAPTER NINE

# World Stars and their Games

During my career I have been lucky enough to play against most of the world's top table tennis players. I have been fortunate too in adding to my knowledge not only by opposing them on the table, but by watching them, and also by discussing the game with most of them.

In this way I have acquired an in-depth understanding of the styles and techniques of these stars. In particular I have been able to pinpoint their strengths, and more important, their weaknesses.

In this chapter I pass on much of this exceedingly useful knowledge by analysing the games of ten of today's top players, three English stars, and that of the best player ever – Chuang Tse-Tung of China.

The ages of the players given here are as at April 1977.

## MITSURU KOHNO of JAPAN
*Age 30. Reigning World Singles Champion.*

Kohno is nicknamed 'sleepy' because of his habit of cat-napping between matches, but in the tournament arena he is the all-action man of table tennis.

He is fleet-footed and muscular like a lightweight boxer and plays a whirlwind pen-hold attacking game from both wings.

He is the complete percentage player going for quick kills without working for openings. This makes it difficult to formulate tactics against him. It is also where his weakness lies. When his timing is slightly off he makes more errors than winners.

Kohno is one of the few modern stars who do not rely on spin. He flat-hits in the old-school style, and uses pimples 'out' on his bat to do so.

Early in his career he was purely a forehand hitter relying on speed to cover the table. In recent years however he has developed an impressive backhand hit.

Mitsuru wears glasses but never appears to have the trouble with them that some players experience. He wipes them carefully before a match with what is said to be a specially treated cloth. From then on they cause him no problems.

In the 1967 world championships in Stockholm he lost in the men's singles final to fellow countryman, N. Hasegawa. Ten years later in Birmingham he became champion. A remarkable example of pertinacity that one can't help but admire.


## PAK YUNG SUN of NORTH KOREA

*Age 19. Reigning and twice World Singles Champion.*
Pak Yung Sun is a petite lady who plays table tennis in the style of a man. She is a left-handed pen-hold player with a powerful forehand.

At times she upsets opponents with her excitable temperament, shouting, squealing, and throwing her arms aloft when she wins a point.

She has a number of weaknesses particularly on her backhand side. These she overcomes with a tigerish fighting spirit, which also often enables her to come from well behind to win games.

In tight situations she displays ice-cool control, no sign of nerves – the hallmark of a champion.

# STELLAN BENGTSSON of SWEDEN

*Age 24. World Singles Champion at Nagoya in 1971. Former European Singles Champion and World Doubles Champion.*

Stellan is a left-handed attacking player. Outside the Chinese he is the best exponent of the third-ball attack manoeuvre in the world.

One of the secrets of his success is the extensive dossiers he keeps on all top players. He knows in advance the type of game his opponent will play. He adapts his game accordingly and capitalizes to the full on any weaknesses.

Bengtsson's consistency puts considerable pressure on his opponents. He gives nothing away, and they really have to win points against him.

Other attributes that helped to make him a world champion are superb footwork, excellent short-game especially against difficult services, and an unflappable temperament.

His weakness is a lack of power. This enables the world's best defenders to defeat him, and those of a lesser calibre to cause him trouble.

He is a crowd pleaser, but such a tough competitor that I find him one of the hardest players to beat.

# DRAGUTIN SURBEK of YUGOSLAVIA

*Age 31. Former European Champion.*

Surbek is exceptional in world-class table tennis in that he relies almost solely on his forehand strength to win games.

He accomplishes this with the aid of a wide variety of spin services and super fitness.

He has the build of a heavyweight boxer, yet because he trains with the work rate of a racehorse, he can move about the arena with the speed of a greyhound.

His forehand loop drive is the equal to any in the world. He plays this shot from almost any part of the table with power and severe spin.

Although Dragutin tends to start slowly he has a big reputation for coming from behind to win games.

Remarkably he has difficulty in 'reading' the spin on the ball. This is one reason for his slow starts. Once into the game his touch and feel for the ball enables him to deal with spin.

At times in doubles matches his partner, Anton Stipancic, aids him by calling out the type of spin that is on the ball.

The obvious weakness in Surbek's game is on his backhand side. Clever opponents exploit this by putting pressure on his backhand in a bid to force him to move around to take the ball with his forehand. They then attempt to spreadeagle him with a quick switch wide to the forehand side.

Surbek is a professional table tennis player and as such is a respected and popular sporting figure in Yugoslavia.


## LIANG KE-LIANG of CHINA
*Age 26. Reigning World Doubles Champion.*
Liang plays with the shake-hands grip, which is unusual for a Chinese. He is equally adept at killing the ball with forehand and backhand.

He was one of the first Chinese players to use the controversial long-pimpled rubber on one side of his bat. With it, Liang baffles his opponents by switching the racket around when serving and defending. Because they are unable to read the spin, this effectively breaks up their games.

Liang is an exceedingly classy player, and two outstanding features of his game are his superlative footwork and lightning reflexes.

It is difficult to pinpoint a weakness in his technique and it is a mystery to me why he has not become world singles champion.

He is in my view the most complete table tennis player playing today.


## JACQUES SECRETIN of FRANCE
*Age 28. Reigning European Singles Champion and World Mixed Doubles Champion.*

Secretin is the supreme table tennis artist. A superbly talented left-hander, he can do almost anything with the ball – spin, control, placements, angles, and subtle changes of pace.

He uses these skills to keep his opponents guessing at all times.

He dictates the play, usually a few paces back from the table. His opponents, no matter what they try, invariably end up playing at the pace Jacques wants them to.

Jacques is at his spectacular best when forced way back from the table and actually wins points from this position – a rare accomplishment. He does so by persistently returning the ball and cleverly changing the spins. This tires his opponents and forces them into making mistakes.

In these circumstances opponents try to beat him with short balls. But such is his mobility I personally have never seen him caught out by a drop shot.

Like other talented artists Secretin is occasionally prone to temperamental lapses and this is his major weakness.

But, when he is on top of his game, he is one of the world's most exciting players to watch.

## NORIO TAKASHIMA of JAPAN
### *Age 25. Former Japanese Champion.*

Takashima is the best defensive player in the world today. He plays the old-style, classical chopping game way back from the table. As with Liang Ke-liang, he uses the shake-hands grip.

He has the reputation of never being caught out by a drop shot.

Norio is an elegant mover, and an artistic stroke player – beautiful to watch.

He was born out of his time. If he had played before the era of big spins he would undoubtedly have been world champion.

In addition to his defensive skills, Takashima has the ability to win points with surprise forehand and backhand smashes.

His weakness is that he cannot cope with the big spins of the top loop-drive specialists.


## KJELL JOHANSSON of SWEDEN
### *Age 31. Three times World Doubles Champion.*
### *Twice European Singles Champion.*

Kjell Johansson is known throughout the table tennis world as the 'Hammer' because of his one hundred miles per hour forehand kill.

He is a pleasure to play against because of his open style, but his persistence and tenacity make him a difficult man to beat.

His basic game is a counter-hitting one interspersed with his famous forehand kill. He employs this on a percentage basis, i.e. although there is an element of risk in the shot he knows that his percentage of winners will be higher than his mistakes.

Unlike many counter-hitters he plays an effective long-range game. Even when forced out of position he has the knack of retrieving the ball, and at times even winning the point with spectacular smashes.

For a tall man, he moves about the arena exceptionally well.

He has the best temperament in the game – nothing ruffles him. This ice-cold composure may owe something to his habit of chewing a quid of tobacco when playing.

His use of close-to-the-table block-shots is masterful. With them he counters even the severest spins with an enviable certainty.

Occasionally he reveals a weakness down the backhand side when under pressure.

Although Kjell fights desperately hard to the last point to win, he does so in the most sporting way. He is a true gentleman of table tennis.


### KUO YAO-HUA of CHINA
*Age 21. Reigning World Doubles Champion.*

Kuo is the first Chinese player to master the modern loop topspin style. Hitherto most Chinese stars have been quick counter-hitters.

His high-thrown serves were the talking point at the 1977 world championships in Birmingham. They made more news when he was faulted in the singles final for using them illegally – this after having passed the scrutiny of numerous umpires in the previous ten days.

Kuo's game is founded on his services and powerful follow-up. These services were so potent at Birmingham that even experienced internationals were made to look like novices when attempting to return them.

With this advantage it is difficult for any opponent to get into the game against him.

The way Kuo plays against defensive players is an object lesson in how to beat them. Such is the power of his first loop – produced with perfect timing – that they find it impossible to return the ball low enough to prevent him killing it.

Kuo differs from most other loopers in that on his backhand he uses the typical Chinese block-push shot.

His weakness is a suspect temperament. This was exposed when he was faulted in the world singles final. In spite of this he is a good prospect to become world champion in the future.


## ISTVAN JONYER of HUNGARY
### Age 26. Former World Champion. Twice World Doubles Champion.

Jonyer at his best can beat any other player in the world. He is the one player the Chinese fear.

Istvan is 'Mr Superspin' of table tennis. He has developed the ability to spin the ball on the forehand and backhand more than any other player in the history of the game.

His rocket forehand loop which bends around the net is his big point winner – virtually unstoppable.

His spins, combined with service excellence, enable him to dictate the way the game is played.

He possesses too that precious quality of champions – time always in which to play his shots.

With these attributes Jonyer should be unbeatable. That he isn't is due to a suspect temperament. He loses concentration without apparent reason, and this accounts for far too many bad losses.

But win or lose, the superbly athletic Hungarian is always a pleasure to watch.

# DESMOND DOUGLAS of ENGLAND
*Age 21. Former English Closed Champion.*
*Reigning English Doubles Champion.*

Des is my England doubles partner and our many successes together include reaching the quarter-finals of the 1977 world championships, and winning three Norwich Union English titles.

He is known as the 'Black Flash' because of his quick footwork and lightning reflexes.

Des is a prime example of a natural player. He plays instinctively with little regard to tactics. Although at times this is to his advantage, he really needs a good tactical captain behind him to produce his best.

He is a left-hander who plays his backhand with awkward angles at speed. This often catches opponents out of position.

He is a master of the close-to-the-table short game.

His big weakness is that he cannot yet change his game when in a losing position.

His temperament has improved over the years but he still has some way to go to become a composed player.

I rate Des among the top five players produced in England in the past twenty-five years.


# JILL HAMMERSLEY of ENGLAND
*Age 25. Reigning European Singles Champion.*

Jill plays the classical, long-range women's defensive game, keeping her returns very low. Any loose balls she puts away with a superbly produced backhand hit.

At present Jill loses to many top Oriental players. This is due to a weakness in her forehand hitting. She tends to snatch at the ball.

Also when defending against slow, looped balls on the forehand side her returns are sometimes too high.

If Jill eliminates these weaknesses she can become world champion.

### CAROLE KNIGHT of ENGLAND
*Age 19. Current holder of the Norwich Union*
*'Open' and 'Closed' Singles titles.*

Carole surged to the forefront of English women's table tennis in 1977 when she won the two major English titles. She beat Jill Hammersley in both finals.

Carole is one of the few girl players to have mastered the men's hitting style.

She hits with power and tremendous topspin, and it is this power that overcomes most of her opponents.

A suspect temperament is her big failing. When the run of the ball isn't with her she frequently loses heart and finds it difficult to fight back.

Signs of an improvement in her fighting spirit were seen at the 1977 world championships when she came within three points of beating the reigning world champion, Pak Yung Sun of North Korea.

If this improvement continues, England will have a world class women's team for years to come.

### CHUANG TSE-TUNG of CHINA
*Retired. Three times World Singles Champion,*
*1961, 1963 and 1965.*

The best player ever! This is my opinion and the opinion of many knowledgeable table tennis experts.

Chuang had everything a table tennis champion should have – perfect temperament, superb fitness, a wide variety of spin services, and the ability to smash the ball as power-fully on the backhand side as on the forehand. No other pen-hold player in the history of the game has matched this hitting prowess.

His was the almost perfect game. He dictated the play no matter what style he was up against. This made it virtually impossible for opponents to be in with a real chance of winning.

Unlike today's Chinese stars whose results are so unaccountably erratic, Chuang was a model of consistency.

He made the mistake of returning to top level competition following a long absence brought about by China's withdrawal from all international sport. Although still a formidable player, inevitably Chuang could not recapture his former brilliance.

Nevertheless a great, great champion!

# The World Ranking List – July 1977
## MEN

| | | |
|---|---|---|
| 1. | Mitsuru Kohno | Japan |
| 2. | Kuo Yao-Hua | PR China |
| 3. | Huang Liang | PR China |
| | Liang Ke-liang | PR China |
| 5. | Dragutin Surbek | Yugoslavia |
| 6. | Jacques Secretin | France |
| 7. | Stellan Bengtsson | Sweden |
| 8. | Istvan Jonyer | Hungary |
| | Milan Orlowski | Czechoslovakia |
| 10. | Gabor Gergely | Hungary |
| 11. | Tibor Klampar | Hungary |
| | Norio Takashima | Japan |
| 13. | Kjell Johansson | Sweden |
| 14. | Li Chen-Shih | PR China |
| 15. | Wilfried Lieck | Germany FR |
| | Anton Stipancic | Yugoslavia |
| 17. | Sarkis Sarkhojan | U.S.S.R. |
| | Tokio Tasaka | Japan |
| 19. | Jochen Leiss | Germany FR |
| 20. | Stanislav Gomozkov | U.S.S.R. |
| 21. | Ulf Thorsell | Sweden |
| 22. | Anatoly Strokatov | U.S.S.R. |
| 23. | Patrick Birocheau | France |
| | Wang Chien-Chiang | PR China |
| 25. | Desmond Douglas | England |
| 26. | Jaroslav Kunz | Czechoslovakia |
| 27. | Peter Stellwag | Germany FR |
| 28. | Tetsuo Inoue | Japan |
| 29. | Zoran Kosanovic | Yugoslavia |
| 30. | Milivoj Karakasevic | Yugoslavia |
| 31. | Christian Martin | France |
| 32. | Denis Neale | England |
| 33. | Li Yu-Hsiang | PR China |
| 34. | Masahiro Maehara | Japan |
| 35. | Danny Seemiller | U.S.A. |
| 36. | Choi Sung Kuk | Korea R |
| 37. | Lee Sang Kuk | Korea R |
| 38. | Li Kuang Tsu | Hong Kong |
| 39. | Katsuyuki Abe | Japan |
| 40. | Paul Day | England |

# The World Ranking List – July 1977
## WOMEN

1. Pak Yung Sung        DPR Korea
2. Chang Li        PR China
3. Chang Te-Ying        PR China
    Ke Hsin-Ai        PR China
5. Chu Hsiang-Yun        PR China
6. Chung Hyun Sook        Korea R
7. Beatrix Kishazi        Hungary
8. Ursula Hirschmuller        Germany FR
9. Ilona Uhlikova        Czechoslovakia
10. Jill Hammersley        England
    Ann-Christin Hellman        Sweden
    Kayoko Kawahigashi        Japan
    Lee Ailesa        Korea R
14. Maria Alexandru        Rumania
15. Sachiko Yokota        Japan
16. Judit Magos        Hungary
17. Ri Song Suk        DPR Korea
18. Elmira Antonian        U.S.S.R.
    Kim Soon Ok        Korea R
    Zoia Rudnova        U.S.S.R.
21. Erzebet Palatinus        Yugoslavia
22. Gabriella Szabo        Hungary
23. Claude Bergeret        France
24. Pak Yong Ok        DPR Korea
25. Tomie Edano        Japan
26. Valentina Popova        U.S.S.R.
27. In-Sook Bhushan        U.S.A.
28. Carole Knight        England
29. Kim Chang Ai        DPR Korea
30. Yen Kuei-Li        PR China
31. Huang Hsi-Ping        PR China
32. Siu Kit Man        Hong Kong
33. Yang Ying        PR China
34. Liana Mihut        Rumania
35. Chang Siu Ying        Hong Kong
36. Blanka Silhavova        Czechoslovakia
37. Wiebke Hendriksen        Germany FR
38. Tatiana Ferdman        U.S.S.R.
39. Eva Ferenczi        Rumania
40. Brigitte Thiriet        France

CHAPTER TEN

# My Prediction

I have often been asked whether or not I think a youngster has it in him to become a table tennis champion – ranked, say, in the top four in England.

It is a question you can never answer with certainty. There are too many unpredictable factors like temperament, and how they will develop physically, and not least whether they possess that indefinable quality that all champions have.

My usual reply, if the player in question looks to have potential, is, 'He looks promising, keep working at it.' This is as far as you can honestly go.

Having said this I am about to put my professional judgement on the line by making a prediction.

The prediction is this: 'By Christmas 1980, fourteen-year-old Graham Sandley, will be ranked in the top four in England and challenging strongly for world honours.'

I make this prediction to demonstrate my confidence in a rare talent.

Graham, from Potters Bar, Hertfordshire, is in my view, the best prospect in England for future table tennis successes.

I have practised with him and I am sure I am right. In one so young it is surprising to find so many of the qualities of a champion that I mentioned earlier in the book, natural flair, will to win, and most important of all, dedication to the game.

In the four years he has been playing, Graham, a left-handed looper, has won fifty-six trophies, and represented England juniors five times.

He will soon be adding to these achievements in what I am convinced will be a rapid rise to the top.

Note the name again, Graham Sandley, follow his career, and see if I am right.

# CHAPTER ELEVEN

# Fitness Training

Physical training programmes for table tennis should be geared to the individual. Each player has different needs and the precise nature of these can only be learned from experience. Until then general guidelines have to be followed and gradually adapted to one's personal requirements.

Training schedules should be drawn up with specific purposes in mind. For instance, 'Are you training for weekend tournaments?, or a fortnight-long world championship? Are you training to improve your stamina?, or to speed up your footwork? Do you need to strengthen particular parts of your body?'

Above all training must be directed at improving the physical attributes used in the game of table tennis. I emphasize this because some physical education experts lose sight of it in their enthusiasm at training just for training's sake.

With these thoughts in mind, here, listed under appropriate headings, are exercises and routines I have found to be of value in my training.


**General Fitness Routines**

During the out-of-season summer months aim to improve the all-round level of your physical fitness. Concentrate on developing strength and stamina.

Try the following routines:

1. A steady three-mile jog three times a week, taking

occasional deep breaths. Don't go for speed but be purposeful in your movements.

2. Use a short, circuit training routine, i.e. repeating a sequence of exercises, usually from six to twelve, one after the other with a brief pause between each.

For each exercise there is a set number of repetitions. When the full series of exercises is completed they are undertaken again – hence the name 'circuit'. Two or three circuits usually constitute a training session.

As one improves in strength and stamina the number of repetitions may be increased, or the overall time taken for the full circuits reduced.

The exercises can include press-ups, sit-ups, double leg jumps, and any of the many varied arm, leg, and trunk movements.

 Always be prepared to work hard at your exercises. Keep in mind the Denis Neale dictum, 'Train hard, play easy!'

3. Weight training with light weights can be of benefit, but where possible do it under the guidance of an expert.

Try these exercises:

(*a*) The Clean. Start with the shins touching the barbell which is on the floor. Bend knees, grasp the bar with both hands, keep your back straight and your head up. Straighten your legs and back smartly, and pull the bar to chest height. Keep it close to the body. As the bar passes the chest, turn the hands over at the wrists so it comes to rest at the shoulders.

To return the weight to the ground, revert your hands to the grasp position, lean slightly forwards, straighten your arms, bend your knees and lower carefully to the floor.

This is an excellent movement for exercising the back and giving the thighs a work-out.

(*b*) Rest the bar across the shoulders, with feet comfortably astride. Bend forward from the hips until the trunk is parallel to the floor. Keep back straight, knees braced back and avoid dropping the head forward. Adopt an erect position immediately. Breathe out as you bend down; in as you straighten up.

(*c*) Lie on your back on a bench or box with the barbell at arms length above your face, palms towards the front. Grip should be narrow. From this position lower barbell to behind the head and back again. Although a little upper arm movement is necessary to enable the bar to clear the head, keep the upper arm as straight as possible.

(*d*) Deep Knee Bends. Breathe in before you descend and let out the air as you rise. The movement should not be too fast but aim for a smooth rhythm.

**Pre-Season Training**
As the playing season approaches in the autumn adapt your training to bring in speed, mobility work, and naturally much more time at the table. Here is a selection of exercises geared to these ends:

(*a*) Really explosive sixty-yard dashes to be repeated after brief intervals. As you progress increase the repetitions to as many as twenty. This is designed to enable you to move at speed right throughout a match.

(*b*) Shadow play at the table. Employ the stroke patterns, body movements, and footwork you use in your game. Be positive and sharp about it. An excellent alternative way to do this is in front of a full-length mirror.

(*c*) Jumping squats. If possible, hold a 10 lb dumb-bell in each hand. Starting position is with your hands by your sides, body and head erect, feet together. Now leap high into the air. As you rise, bring your knees up to your chest and back again as you go down into a full deep knee bend. Take a deep breath before you leap and breathe out as you perform the movement. The exercise is tough, but can be made less so by excluding the deep knee bend part of it.

(*d*) Back stretch with leg raised. Rest your left foot on a box or bench at about right angles to your upright body. Keeping your legs straight, grasp the ankle of your left leg and pull gently in an effort to touch your knee with your chin. Because of restricted mobility in the lower back, it may not be possible at first even to grasp hold of your ankle. Don't worry. Hold as low down as possible. Flexibility will come with persistence. Repeat the exercise with the right leg raised.

 Where possible exercise to music to relieve any tedium and help the rhythm along. I do so to the theme music from the film *The Sting*. This was recommended to me by Ken Woolcott who organizes 'Pop-Mobility' training.

**Additional Exercises for Wrists and Ankles**

(*a*) Tie a piece of cord eighteen inches long to a three-foot-long piece of wood – a section of a broom handle is ideal. Attach a 10 lb weight to the string. Simply wind up until all the string is wound around the wood, then unwind.

Make it a steady winding movement and make sure the wrists and forearms do the work. Keep the upper arms close to the body moving neither forwards or backwards: keep the forearms at right angles.

(*b*) Here's another excellent wrist strengthener. Sit on a stool or bench with your forearms resting against the thighs. The palms of your hands should be facing upwards and you should grasp a barbell firmly. The hands should project beyond the knees. The movement is simple yet effective. Raise and lower the barbell by hand movement alone. Now repeat with palms down.

71

(*c*) In a standing position, take your weight on your left leg and lift your right leg off the ground. Go up on the toes of your left foot and then sink into a full deep knee bend, making sure you keep your left heel off the floor. Repeat six times with the same leg without placing your right foot on the floor. Repeat the exercise with the weight this time on the toes of your right foot. Rest hands lightly on a chair or against a wall to assist balance.

(*d*) Support yourself on a chair or against a wall and lift one foot off the ground. Bend the toes of the other leg towards your shin. Maintaining this position, turn the foot outwards and then inwards. It is important that the entire foot be moved, as one unit. Simply twisting the toes is useless. Repeat outwards and inwards twenty times and then perform the movement with the other foot.

**Exercises at the Table**
A selection of pattern-play exercises appear in the chapter on stroke production. They can be adapted for your fitness training programmes.

More table exercises are included in the descriptions of international training routines that follow.

## AT AN ENGLAND TRAINING CAMP

Training camps for England teams are held throughout the year, often at Lea Green Recreation Centre, near Matlock, Derbyshire.

The training programme at each camp is prepared according to the time of year and the proximity to big matches or a major championship.

A typical day's time-table is:

8 a.m. Rise. 8.30. Breakfast. 9.15. Warm-up. 9.30. Service practice. 10.30. Break. 11.00. Stroke and pressure play practice. 1 p.m. Lunch. 2.15. Warm-up. 2.30. Stroke practice or competitive play. 3.45. Break. 4.00. More stroke

practice or doubles play. 6.30. Dinner. 8.00. Discussion time and film analysis with the aid of video-tapes. 10.30. Bed.

## The Warm-up

The following pre-play warm-up routine is ideal for loosening up, and easing the tension from muscles, before matches and tournaments.

At the camps we carry it out in a group under the direction of a leader. Nicky Jarvis, the England star, with his zest for physical exercise, is an inspiration in this role.

## Running Movements

Jog around the hall (or outside). Breathe deeply and try to relax your muscles. Then, still jogging, include these variations:

(a) A couple of really explosive short sprints.
(b) Some sideways skipping.
(c) Run backwards for a few yards, well up on your toes.
(d) Stop running and jogging. Instead walk briskly for the duration of five very deep breaths.

This should last about five minutes.

## Table Tennis Movements

Perform each movement fifteen times:

(a) Low side shuttles. Stay low and move easily back-hand to forehand, moving only sideways. Touch floor each time with the playing hand.
(b) Knee turns. Hands on hips, feet astride. Drop into a form of deep knee bend, but twist the trunk as you go down, so that your knee comes over and touches the floor – right knee on your left side, left knee on your right side. Come up to the upright position after each individual movement.

(c) Side jumps. Push off from the outside leg and land in a crouched position. Repeat off alternate legs. The aim is to travel longways and not upwards.

These movements should take no more than about three minutes.

**Mobility Movements**

(a) Shake wrist vigorously and stretch and curl fingers. Repeat with each hand until wrists and fingers are relaxed and loose.

(b) Lock fingers in front of you and move your arms sideways, left and then right. Keep fingers locked, wrists and elbows together.

(c) Circle arms four or five times forwards. Repeat backwards. Swing loosely from the shoulder and bring arms right over through 360 degrees.

(d) Roll neck and head, side to side, up and down, and in a complete circular movement both ways.

(e) Side lever. Keep body upright. Bend over sideways, stretching one arm down the leg. The other arm curls up under the armpit.

(f) Trunk circling. Standing position with arms above head. Bend down forwards until the trunk is at right angles. Circle trunk round through 360 degrees. Five times each way.

(g) Touching toes with feet astride. Right hand to left foot; left hand to right foot.

(h) Splits. Alternate legs forward, easing down to stretch the ligaments. Don't strain, but attempt a deeper split each exercise session.

(i) Side-splits. Similar position, but on one leg. Hands on the stretched leg, pushing downwards.

The entire warm-up routine takes from ten to fifteen minutes.

**Exercises at the Table**

Each exercise is clearly defined and meticulously practised.

(a) A counter-hitting routine carried out in fifteen-minute sequences and, allowing for breaks, lasting for one hour thirty minutes, is: Forehand to forehand; Backhand to backhand; Forehand to backhand; Backhand to forehand; Random counter-hitting.

(b) The third-ball attack manoeuvre is played in the form of a game. One player serves continuously throughout the game. He has to win each point with two shots, i.e. service and follow-up stroke. If he does not he loses the point. Next game the roles are reversed.

This is a frequently encountered match-play situation. The pressure is on to serve well and to return service with matching skill.

(c) Stamina is catered for in a pressure-play exercise lasting fifteen minutes.

A feeder throws one hundred balls, one after the other, to the player. The object is for him to keep on killing them with full power.

Initially you begin to tire early, but with regular practice you succeed in sustaining full power to the end.

This is often a vital factor in matches. Being able to sustain the pressure right up to the final points can clinch the issue for you.

**Video Tapes**

Video film aids are used at the England training camps and prove invaluable in analysing your own game, and those of your team mates.

Studying the styles and techniques of the world stars on film is another rewarding exercise.

## Yoga

A recent addition to the English camp routine is Yoga. This is practised at the end of the day to try and induce complete relaxation. It is a specialized field and I am undecided as to its usefulness in a table tennis context.

## AT A YUGOSLAV TRAINING CAMP

I spent two weeks at a camp in Yugoslavia training with their top players, including Dragutin Surbek and pen-holder Melevoy Karakasevic. With me were Jill Hammersley and Trevor Taylor.

The training was conducted with military precision and discipline. The accent was on heavy physical activity – lots of roadwork and stamina training routines, broken up with games of football and basketball.

Surbek, the Yugoslav dynamo, put in an astonishing amount of work. He was still going strong when the rest of us were wilting.

Exercise periods were timed to match the playing schedules of a world championship. Likewise, the playing areas simulated the conditions to be found at a world or European championship – similar dimensions, surrounds, umpires' desks and scoring equipment. You felt as if you were actually playing in a top event.

## Films

Films of actual matches were analysed and compared with video tapes of practise play. This is a useful aid in correcting slight errors of technique, and alerting you to the over-use of stroke patterns so preventing your game becoming stereotyped.

**Relaxation**

At the end of a day's exercise all the players relaxed on the floor of a darkened room. A doctor spoke to us in a low modulated voice for twenty minutes. It was soothing and relaxing, and I felt refreshed afterwards.

**Conclusion**

I think Yugoslav training methods are first rate, and I certainly benefited from them. But I do prefer a little more flexibility in arrangements, and a little less regimentation.

## JAPANESE TRAINING

Much of the training for table tennis in Japan is directed at building up stamina and power. I found out why when I played their world champions, S. Itoh, N. Hasegawa and M. Kohno.

They are human dynamos who burn up energy by attacking and applying pressure to their opponents from the first point to the last.

Their play is intensely physical, and so is their training as I learned when touring Japan with a European all-stars side.

The training schedules are heavy and incorporate extensive use of weights and circuit routines.

**Exercises**

Many of their exercises are similar to those I have already outlined, but there are variations.

Here are some used in a typical Japanese programme:

**Exercises for Abdominal Muscles**

(1) Lie stretched out flat on the floor, on your back. From this position perform thirty half sit-ups.
(2) From the same position hold both legs six inches off the floor for one minute. Repeat five times.

(3) Perform the half sit-ups with a dumb-bell weighing from 2 lbs to 6 lbs in each hand. Do this ten times then rest. Repeat the sequence five times.

(4) Squat jumps. From a squatting position, bound forwards, sideways, or backwards for a distance of thirty yards. Increase the distance when you become proficient.

Circuit routines are built up from a combination of these movements and others such as press-ups, and jumping on the spot.

Remember the number of repetitions for these exercises are suggestions only and can be varied to suit the individual.

## Finger Pulling and Palm Pressing

With fingers together and bent towards the palms, interlock the fingertips. Attempt to pull your hands apart, forcing the fingers against each other. Keep the pressure up for thirty to sixty seconds.

For palm pressing bring the heels of the hands together. Push them hard together for from thirty to sixty seconds.

## Side Step

Start in a low crouch as if ready to play, legs about a yard apart and arms extended in front for balance. Slide the left leg quickly in towards the right, transfer your weight and move the right leg out to the side as you return to the crouch position. Next reverse the procedure.

Repeat the exercise thirty times.

## Wrist Exercise

Hold a dumb-bell weighing from one to two pounds in your playing hand and move the wrist in various directions. This can be done in a tub of warm water.

Take care not to overdo this exercise.

**Shadow Play**

Hold a bat or a light weight and swing your racket arm from five hundred to one thousand times. Then outline your strokes in shadow play preferably with the use of a mirror.

The Japanese schedule concludes with two sensible pieces of advice. 'It is more effective to exercise regularly, little by little, than to cram a lot in at one time', and 'Table tennis techniques can benefit only to limited degree from sheer physical strength'.


## CHINESE TRAINING

Observe any Chinese squad training and two qualities stand out – discipline and dedication. Their coaches seemingly only have to raise a finger to obtain immediate attention and obedience.

They have, I believe, developed training methods to such a degree that it is now practically a science. Their success at world level, where the Chinese reign supreme as team champions, is proof that their methods work.


**Chinese Coach**

Here are some ideas put forward by a leading Chinese coach.

Hard work and seriousness in training are vital if a player is to progress.

Use your brain in training as you would in playing.

Be systematic and have a particular end in view. For instance, if your reactions need sharpening, exercise with this in mind. Running and changing direction on a given signal is one way to do this.

Each player should have a training programme designed specifically for them.

**Chinese Warm-up Exercises**

The following exercises should last from fifteen to twenty minutes.

A rhythmic count up to eight helps them along and an authentic touch can be achieved by using Chinese numerals. 1 EE. 2 AH. 3 SUN. 4 CE. 5 WU. 6 LEO. 7 CHI. 8 BA.

The purpose of the exercises is to prepare the muscles for the playing action to come.

(1) Run three or four times around the playing arena depending on the size.

(2) Continue running in a smaller circle with a high knee action.

(3) Run sideways, facing in, change on a signal and face out. Repeat the changes.

(4) Occasionally while running use the scissors cross-over step.

(5) Commence arm rotating exercises with shoulders first forwards, then backwards. Do so to the rhythm of the eight count.

(6) With arms at shoulder height, elbows bent, stretch in front of the chest then fling the arms outwards.

(7) Raise one arm sideways over the head, pushing the other arm behind the back. Then reverse the arm movements.

(8) Raise your arms high and stretch upwards. Then bend and touch the floor.

(9) With arms half bent in front of you rotate the trunk from the waist keeping your feet firmly on the floor.

(10) Leg-stretching. With front leg bent, back leg extended backwards. Count to eight and then reverse leg positions.

(11) Leg-stretching in a similar way, but sideways.

(12) Knee circling.

(13) Toe grinding.

(14) Head rolling.

THE READY POSITION

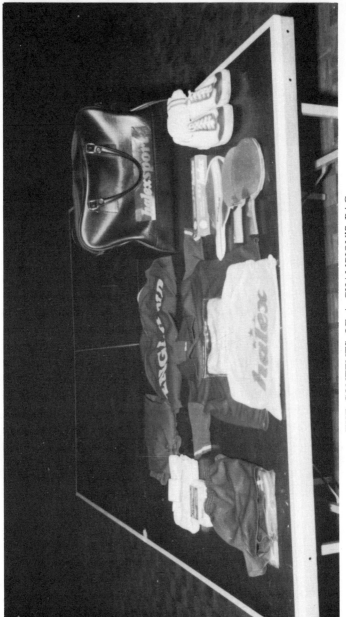

THE CONTENTS OF A CHAMPION'S BAG

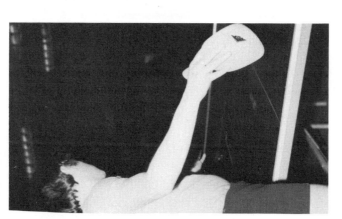

## PENHOLD GRIP

*Top right:*
Forehand view.

*Left:*
Backhand view.

The more usual handshake grip is shown in the other photographs.

Backhand side spin.

Forehand side spin.

SERVES

Forehand high throw up.

Backswing.

Near contact.

FOREHAND TOPSPIN DRIVE

Follow through.

Follow through.

Near contact.

FOREHAND LOOP TOPSPIN

Preparation.

Preparation.

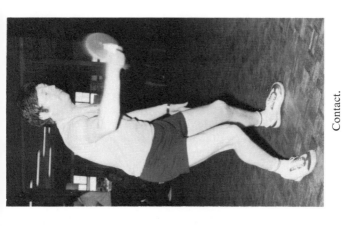

Contact.

## BACKHAND LOOP TOPSPIN

Follow through.

THE SCISSOR-KICK KILL

Three positions.

FLAT FOREHAND KILL

*Above:* Backswing.

*Right:* Follow through.

BACKHAND COUNTER-HIT

*Top*: Preparation.

*Centre*: Near contact.

*Right*: Follow through.

FOREHAND PUSH

BACKHAND PUSH

Follow through.

Contact.

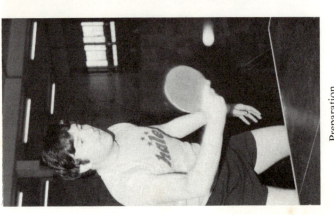

Preparation.

BACKHAND BLOCK SHOT

## Body Exercises

These include:

(1) Push-ups.

(2) Sit-ups with hands behind the head and with a partner holding the ankles firmly; bend forward to reach the knees with the head.

(3) Long squat jumps; stoop and spring forward.

(4) Stand with your back to a wall, about a yard away. Without moving your feet reach back placing your palms flat against the wall. Do this alternately, then simultaneously. This is good for the waist and shoulders.

(5) Lie on your back, raise your legs and arms simultaneously to touch.

(6) Use bars for pull-ups.

(7) Run up and down stairs.

(8) Skipping.

## Loosening-up Routines

(For use after the body exercises.)

(1) Hop on one leg while shaking the other.

(2) Swing loosely from the waist.

(3) Swing arms while raising legs alternately.

## Chinese Table Exercises

1. Forehand counter-hitting . . . 20 minutes.

2. Backhand counter-hitting . . . 20 minutes.

3. Backhand counter-hitting and forehand smash from the backhand side . . . 20 minutes.

4. Rest for 15 minutes.

5. Serve and smash return . . . 20 minutes.

6. Return of service . . . 20 minutes.

7. Chop, chop, then turn and loop either fast or slow . . . 20 minutes.

8. Rest for 15 minutes.

9. Push, push, and loop drive . . . 20 minutes.

10. Chop, chop, and turn on the spot and loop any-

where; then move over to the forehand court and smash
. . . 20 minutes.
11. Two or three competitive games.
12. End with a game of basketball.

## FITNESS TRAINING – CONCLUSION

My suggestion is to try out the exercises I have described
in the preceding pages, adopting those suitable to you, and
discarding those that are not.

Formulate your own training programmes but always
be flexible. Think about your training and be receptive to
new ideas. Training for table tennis is still open for
development.

# CHAPTER TWELVE

# How I Prepare for Big Matches

When training for a particular match or tournament the object is to strike your best form at exactly the right time.

Each player is different and has to work out for themselves how best to prepare for the big occasions. Usually only experience and experiment can tell you this.

My methods have varied over the years. At one time before the English Closed Championships I used to practise solidly for seven days right up to the night before the event. I needed the action to keep me from thinking too much about the English title.

Nowadays, with the benefit of experience, I am more flexible.

During a season, as a top player, I am playing nearly every day. It is impossible in these circumstances to play at one's peak all the time. What I aim to do is to maintain a high enough standard to win, even if I only just manage to do so. If I drop below this standard I know it is time for a change. So I either increase my work-rate in practice, or have a few days complete break from the game.

Before the 1977 Norwich Union English Closed Championships I was going through a lean spell and I knew I had to take some drastic action to snap myself out of the doldrums. I decided to have four days complete rest, and to change to a reserve bat.

This worked wonders for me. I went to the championships thoroughly refreshed and played my best table tennis of the season. I won the singles title for a record sixth time.

At a tournament, or before any big match, I always go through the warm-up routine described in the previous chapter. This not only tones up the muscles but, by giving you something positive to do, helps to settle the nerves that all players have.

Next I try for at least one hour's knock-up to get my shots going and to acclimatise myself to the conditions.

At a tournament I check the draw to see who my opponents are likely to be. I also make a note of the playing schedule so I know the best time to take a light meal.

In this way I give myself every possible chance to win. I strongly recommend all players to do the same.

# CHAPTER THIRTEEN

# Doubles

## Advice for Beginners

In table tennis doubles, unlike other racket games, you have to play the ball alternately with your partner.

You also always have to serve from the right-hand court to the diagonally opposite court. This is why the table is divided into halves by a 3 mm broad white line, running parallel to the sidelines.

Full details of how to score, and the service order, is given in the laws which appear at the rear of the book.

## The Partnership Game

In doubles a left- and right-handed combination is often found to be the most effective pairing. This is because it is much easier for such a duo to play their forehand shots.

I have won several English men's doubles titles with left-handed partners Alan Hydes and Des Douglas.

## Serving

It is essential to serve short most of the time in doubles. This gives your partner more time to cover the table.

Many players use a system of hand signals below the table to indicate to each other the type of service they intend to use. For instance one finger pointed at the floor can mean a short, chopped service; two fingers, a fast, deep service. Others prefer to whisper their intentions.

## Movements

A well-organized pattern of movements is vital to successful doubles play. The prime aim is not to impede each other.

The two traditional ways of moving are equally effective. They are (1) a circulating, clockwise movement; (2) the in and out method, i.e. moving forwards and backwards.

Give your partner more room in which to move by not standing too square-on to the table. Similarly play your shots as economically as possible. If you lunge around you may get in your partner's way, or obstruct his view.

## Styles

The best singles players do not necessarily make the best doubles team. The right blend of styles usually serves to achieve this.

In my view players with similar styles form the best partnerships, and with today's spin two attackers are the best combination.

This is born out at top level where the big majority of doubles players are hitters.

When two players of differing styles play together each should be prepared to modify their game to fit in with that of their partner.

This happens when I play mixed doubles with European champion, Jill Hammersley. I am a quick hitter and Jill is a defensive player with a fine backhand hit.

In order to give Jill the chance to use her attacking shots I take a step back from the table to try and slow the game down.

## Tactics

Work out general tactics with your partner trying to make the best use of your strong points, and minimizing your weaknesses.

For instance if one player has a superior kill, work together as a team to bring this into operation. Of if your partner has difficulty in playing against heavy chops, don't feed your opponents with shots likely to be returned with severe backspin.

Remember variations of pace and direction are as important in doubles play as in singles.

Hitting twice to a previously designated spot on the table and then switching direction is a good move designed to catch opponents out of position. I have used this tactic successfully with my doubles partners in many international doubles matches.

Angled hitting has also been used to good effect. We do so to a pre-arranged plan which has been practised over and over again.

Another sensible move is to identify the weaker of your two opponents and to play on him ruthlessly. Harass him by going for as many winners against him as possible. This can effectively upset the opposition's rhythm.

Keep in mind when making your shots that it is your partner, and not you, who must receive the return. It is so easy to play your normal singles game and find that your shot has been returned awkwardly for your partner. The aim is to play in such a way that you bring out the best in him.

A few words of praise and encouragement can work wonders in this direction too!

 Practise doubles regularly with your usual partner. The more you do the more you will develop that close understanding and teamwork necessary for successful doubles play.

# CHAPTER FOURTEEN

# My View of the 1977 World Championships

The World Table Tennis Championships held at the National Exhibition Centre in Birmingham from March 26th to April 5th were the thirty-fourth of a series that began in 1926. They were the sixth in my personal series.

Approximately five hundred players from over fifty countries took part.

## Conditions

The playing arenas, and a sports and leisure exhibition called 'Sportacus', were accommodated in a gigantic, hangar-like structure which could easily have housed a fleet of airships.

There were twenty tables for the competition and twenty more in the practice area.

For the first time in my experience the championships were staged in two arenas. One contained sixteen tables, the other, where most of the important matches were played, had just four.

This arrangement made it difficult for spectators to watch all the matches they wanted to and I heard several strong criticisms on this score.

Playing conditions in the four-table arena were good considering the centre had not been constructed especially for sporting events. The lighting, installed no doubt to television specifications, was excellent.

This was not the case in the bigger playing arena where the lighting was decidedly inferior – yet another reason why using two arenas is not a good idea. Playing conditions for all matches in a world championship should be as near equal as they can be made.

## Playing Developments

The championships are held every two years and provide the only real opportunity to assess the game as a whole – to study the latest playing trends and developments. It is the one time when all the world's best players are in competition against each other.

What, then, was to be learned at Birmingham? I have referred throughout the book to changes in technique and playing methods, but it is worthwhile adding some more observations about them.

Without doubt the most devastating development in the playing field was the use by some Chinese players, of the new long-pimpled rubber.

I have previously described how this is used and I am glad the laws have changed regarding rubbers (see Laws). I feel so strongly about the rubber because it is not a fair test of sporting endeavour. When I played against it it was the only time in my career I have felt completely at sea when playing my shots.

## Services

The service technique of the Chinese has been developed to a high degree of skill and spectacular elevation. Their high-thrown serves are now being copied around the world. They are not new, having been used intermittently throughout table tennis history, but not with the effectiveness achieved by the Chinese. This serves to underline the scope there is for imaginative development and improvement throughout the full range of table tennis skills.

The 'third-ball attack' tactic was a big feature of play, and service skill was the major factor in this routine of 'service, return of service, and follow-up shot'.

## Defence

More top-class defensive players were seen at Birmingham than in recent world championships, but they were still very much in the minority. It was the hitters who won the titles.

## Oriental Dominance

Before the championships it could be argued that the playing strength of the West was on a par with that of the East. The men's singles champion was Hungarian, and the men's doubles title was held by the same country. To counterbalance this, China held the team titles. The top forty men in the world rankings were evenly divided between the Orient and the Occident.

In the women's rankings, China and Korea were in the ascendant.

After the championships it was clear that the world's best players are largely from the Orient, and mainly pen-holders. China won both team events. Mitsuru Kohno of Japan was the men's singles champion, and Pak Yun Sung of North Korea was once more the ladies' champion. The West received a consolation prize when the mixed doubles title was won by Jacques Secretin and Claude Bergeret of France.

Why this dominance by the East, and in particular, China? If there is one reason it must be dedication. Evidence to support this conclusion could be seen every day at Birmingham in the practice area – it was always full of Chinese, training and practising with zest and obvious enthusiasm.

## The Daily Routine

The day begins at the championships with a call at 8 o'clock. Breakfast is taken and the newspapers scoured for table tennis stories. They sometimes provoke loud laughter.

The bus ride to the arena takes forty minutes. We launch into a physical training session straight away. This is followed by one hour's practice. After this, if a match is due, the non-playing captain announces the team.

After lunch there is more practice, and either an afternoon match or one in the evening.

Between matches, and practice sessions, and meals, there is constant behind-the-scenes activity. Hundreds of people are making demands on your time; friends, supporters and officials. Then there are the media men. They are there in force and if you are the 'man of the moment' you are in demand for press, radio and television interviews. The Fleet Street men are there, as they have been 'there' with you at top events around the world. You are glad to say 'Hello' to, and provide copy for, Roy Moor of the *Daily Mail*, Sydney Hulls of the *Daily Express*, Dickie Rutnagur of the *Daily Telegraph*, Steve Whiting of the *Sun*, and their colleagues.

Then comes a match. Before it begins there is a briefing about the opposition. The team is reminded of weaknesses in the opposing side and possible tactics to adopt against them.

The match begins. Your turn comes to play and you are out on your own in the arena.

This is the time when those grinding hours of practice pay dividends. You don't have time to think about the techniques of shot-making, or the way you move. You just do it by instinct, the way you have done it ten thousand times and more in training.

Experience now comes to your aid and enables you to blot out the activity from adjacent arenas; the loudspeaker announcements; and the sudden eruption of the crowd as they cheer a spectacular point elsewhere. You blot it out and concentrate only on your match.

All the while you are thinking about the play and the general strategy of the game. But you are aware of a hundred and one details – the umpire calling the score, the scorers operating their indicators, shouts of encouragement from your team mates, the expression on your opponent's face . . . all the activity in your arena.

You play hard, and savour the joy of victory, or the resignation of defeat.

### England's Performance
'Disappointing' is the word that sums up England's performance at Birmingham. All the players gave one hundred per cent effort, but the lack of success demonstrates once again that there is something wrong in English table tennis.

I put this down to deficiencies in our coaching and training methods. Until we change the system and introduce new ideas we won't improve our standing in world table tennis.

### Too Big
I believe that the World Table Tennis Championships have now become too big, too unwieldy, and too expensive.

It is becoming increasingly difficult to find countries to stage them.

A radical change is needed, possibly with the championships being run on lines similar to those of World Cup football.

# CHAPTER FIFTEEN

## Hopes for the Future

After nineteen years in table tennis I still retain my enthusiasm for the game.

If it was possible I would start out again tomorrow on a table tennis career.

If I were to do so I would be hoping for some big changes in the game in England.

I would want to see the club system, so successful in Holland, Sweden and Germany, instituted in England. In these countries, clubs are sponsored by commercial concerns and players are much better off financially than the majority are here.

I would be looking for a complete overhaul of our coaching and training methods.

I would be campaigning for a much more professional approach to the sport by those who run it, and all those who play it at top level.

And with any luck I would be studying a publication very similar to *Halex Book of Modern Table Tennis* by Denis Neale. This would speed my progress (as I trust it will yours) and stimulate me to 'Train hard, play easy'.

# Proficiency Awards

The Halex proficiency awards, bronze, silver and gold, included here provide the opportunity for players to assess their standards of play, and the progress they are making.

## Halex Proficiency Award – Bronze Standard

1. All backhand push control:
   (from 2 points, returned to 1 target)
   Using sound footwork for training, return 40 slow push shots (which have been placed, slowly, by the Controller from B, alternately to area C and area D). Candidate to use only backhand push strokes, all played back to area B. (See diagram for the areas.)
   Required: 40 successes before 6th error.
2. All forehand slow topspin roll:
   Against gentle returns from the controller, play 40 roll strokes, maintaining direction on one diagonal only, without increasing speed.
   Required: As test 1.
3. Combined control:
   Return 40 slow balls from the controller by playing, in strict alternation, backhand push and forehand roll, while maintaining direction on one diagonal only.
   Required: As test 1.
4. Backhand block returns:
   Against medium topspin from the controller, return the ball by simple rebound technique, i.e. straight line

'reflection', from the peak-of-bounce position. Maintain direction of one diagonal.

Required: As test 1.

5. Short touch services:
   (a) From correct position behind the baseline, serve short forehand service so as to bounce twice in opponent's court.
   (b) As (a) but service with backhand.

   Required: 4 successes to be achieved within 8 attempts.

6. Long topspin services:
   (a) From correct position, serve with forehand; the ball has to land within 45 cm of distant baseline.
   (b) As (a) but service with backhand.

   Required: 5 successes within 8 attempts.


*Notes:*
   (i) For 'penholder' styles, for backhand read 'to left of body'.
   (ii) For left-handers, reverse targets (A for B, etc.).
   (iii) Two players may be tested simultaneously on one table by using opposite diagonal channel on all above tests except 1.


### Halex Proficiency Award – Silver Standard

*Preliminary:*

Candidates must have passed the Bronze tests.

Before scoring each test, the Assessor shall require:

(a) A 'dry land' demonstration of the ensuing stroke actions.

(b) That the quality of the practical stroke work is satisfactory.

1. Return of service by half volley:
   (a) Using backhand half volley touch, return safely

95

10 services, varied as to topspin and chop and sidespin.

(*b*) As (*a*) but using forehand half volley touch.

Required: 20 successes (10–10) before 6th error.

2. Combining drive and push, forehand:

Return 40 balls which have been alternately pushed and chopped, by using (respectively) topspin drives and push shots, played alternately, forehand, on one diagonal.

Required: 40 correct before 6th error.

3. Combining drive and push, backhand:

As 2 but using backhand throughout.

Required: As test 2.

4. Combining (chopped) defensive returns with push – forehand:

Return 40 balls which have been alternately driven and pushed, on same line, by using, respectively, backspin defensive returns and pushes, played alternately on same line – all forehand.

Required: As test 2.

5. Combining (chopped) defensive returns with push – backhand: As 4 but using backhand throughout.

Required: As test 2.

6. Laws, rules, etc.:

Answer 10 'everyday' questions on laws and match procedure. Points allowed: complete answer: 3; correct 'sense': 2; part answer: 1.

Pass score: 22 out of 30.

7. Maintaining attack against topspin from controller:

(*a*) Maintain 10 triple sequences thus: 2 forehand drives plus 1 backhand block.

Required: 10 good sequences before 5th error.

(*b*) As (*a*) but sequences of: 2 backhand drives plus 1 forehand block.

Required: As test 7(*a*).

8. Services variations:
   Deliver 10 services of varying length, incorporating sidespin, alternately left and right.
   3rd error fails.

### Halex Proficiency Award – Gold Standard

*Preliminary:*
Candidates must have passed the Silver tests.

Candidates must have the approval of an E.T.T.A. Staff Coach or E.T.T.A. Approved Instructor as to general level of playing ability and presentation.

1. Topspin driving under pressure – forehand:
   Play 50 forehand topspin drives, to one point, against half volley returns which have been placed alternately to areas C and D. Good forehand position and footwork required throughout.
   Required: 50 correct before 5th error.
2. Topspin driving under pressure – backhand:
   As 1 but using backhand topspin drives.
   Required: As test 1.
3. Counter driving, close and distant – forehand:
   Return 20 counter drives by means of forehand counter drives in sequences of 2 thus: 2 'close', 2 'distant', 2 'close', etc. All returns kept on same line.
   3rd error fails.
4. Counter driving close and distant – backhand:
   As 3 but using backhand counter drives.
   3rd error fails.
5. Combining forehand and backhand topspin drives:
   Against slow chopped returns, which have been placed alternately to areas J and K, by playing 20 forehand and backhand topspin drives, alternately, directed diagonally to areas F and G.
   3rd error fails.

97

6. Combining forehand and backhand defensive returns backspin:
   Return 20 drives, received alternately on corner areas J and K, by means of, respectively, forehand and backhand chopped returns, to area L.
   3rd error fails.
7. Sequences of topspin and backspin strokes:
   Play 15 double sequences of forehand chop and backhand drive against balls which have been driven to the forehand and pushed to the backhand.
   4th error fails.
8. Sequences of topspin and backspin strokes:
   Play the reverse of 7, i.e. 'backhand' for 'forehand' (and vice versa).
   4th error fails.
9. Backhand attack distribution:
   Play 10 triple sequences thus: dropshot to area E; backhand drive to area F; backhand drive to area G; and repeat. The controller returns all balls to area H, from long distance, with backspin.
   4th error fails.
10. Loop topspin forehand:
    Candidate to demonstrate loop drive 5 times against chopped returns of suitable length and strength, to suit his requirements. The aim is to show understanding of the loop technique, and a continuity of loop drives is not demanded.

### Halex Proficiency Award

*Notes Regarding Assessment:*

1. Candidates should be allowed to warm up.
2. If only one item is failed, a second attempt at that item may be made the same day. If two items are failed, or one failed twice, a new application must be made for a

re-test. A re-test may not be granted within one month of the failed test.

3. Bronze and Silver standards may be taken on the same occasion.

4. Assessors are responsible for arranging: (i) suitable controllers to give each candidate a fair chance, and (ii) a scorer, to keep count of successes and errors.

5. The controller should be a player able to place slow and steady balls to the required targets, with required spin. Mistakes by the controller, or unlucky balls, or balls which are not appropriate to the required test skill, will not be counted against the candidate.

6. Assessors will rule on quality of performance appropriate to each test level. A warning and explanation should be given to any candidate who does not appear to have understood the precise requirements of any test.

A push shot is a return which is low, slow and straight, with a trace of backspin.

7. Appropriate target areas are shown in the test diagram. Since the aim of Proficiency Awards is to train players to maintain control of length and direction, the Assessor should require good consistency in these respects, but allow for difficulties caused by inconsistent 'feeding' from the controller, or difficult playing conditions. If the exchange becomes difficult, it is fairer to call a 'let', and re-start from the score already reached.

8. Marking of the table: A, B, C, D, are centre points of the four 'courts'. Target areas may be regarded as a 'notional' 45 cm square. They need not be marked out in full; for practical purposes, the markers in the diagram provide a sufficient check on the length and directional control of the returns.

9. Assessors should inform candidates of their decisions

and notify results to the Awards Organizer on the blue assessment form (No. 6811) which is obtainable from him at 71 Maplin Way, Thorpe Bay, Essex.

10. Bronze Awards may be assessed by: teachers; league officials; E.T.T.A. coaches or students.

11. Silver Awards must be assessed by E.T.T.A. coaches.

12. Gold Awards will only be assessed at formal sessions organized by the E.T.T.A. and must be approved by a Staff Coach or an E.T.T.A. Approved Instructor.

13. Parents may not assess their own children above Bronze level.

# Halex Proficiency Awards
## TARGET AREAS
### Controller's End

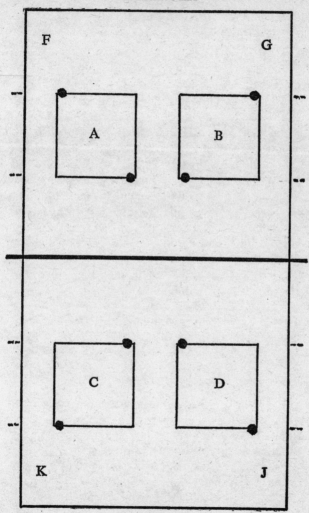

Candidate's End

# Laws

**The Laws of Table Tennis**
## 1. *The Table*
The table shall be in surface rectangular, 274 cm in length and 152·5 cm in width; it shall be supported so that its upper surface, termed the 'playing surface', shall lie in a horizontal plane 76 cm above the floor. It shall be made of any material and shall yield a uniform bounce of not less than 22 cm and not more than 25 cm when a standard ball is dropped from a height of 30·5 cm above its surface. The playing surface shall be dark coloured, preferably dark green, and matt, with a white line 2 cm broad along each edge. The lines at the 152·5 cm edges, or ends, shall be termed 'end lines' and the lines at the 274 cm edges, or sides, shall be termed 'side lines'.

For doubles, the playing surface shall be divided into halves by a white line 3 mm broad, running parallel to the side lines, termed the 'centre line'. The centre line may, for convenience, be permanently marked in full length on the table and this in no way invalidates the table for singles play.

## 2. *The Net and its Supports*
The playing surface shall be divided into two courts of equal size by a net running parallel to the end lines. The net with its suspension, shall be 183 cm in length; along its whole length its upper part shall be 15·25 cm above the playing surface and its lower part shall be close to the playing surface. It shall be suspended by a cord attached at

each end to an upright post 15·25 cm high; the outside limits of each post shall be 15·25 cm outside the side line.

## 3. *The Ball*

The ball shall be spherical, with a diameter of not less than 37·2 mm and not more than 38·2 mm. It shall be made of celluloid or a similar plastic, white or yellow, and matt; it shall be not less than 2·40 gm and not more than 2·53 gm in weight.

## 4. *The Racket*

The racket may be of any size, shape or weight. The blade shall be of wood, continuous, of even thickness, flat and rigid and each side shall be uniformly dark-coloured.

If a side of the blade used for striking the ball is covered, this covering, which shall extend over the whole striking surface, shall be either ordinary 'pimpled rubber', with pimples outwards, having a total thickness, including adhesive, of not more than 2 mm, or 'sandwich rubber', with pimples inwards or outwards, having a total thickness including adhesive of not more than 4 mm.

'Pimpled rubber' is a layer of non-cellular rubber, with pimples evenly distributed over its surface at a density of not less than 10/sq cm and not more than 50/sq cm.

'Sandwich rubber' is a layer of cellular rubber surfaced with a layer of pimpled rubber, the total thickness of the pimpled rubber being not more than 2 mm.

If a side of the blade used for striking the ball is not covered, the wood shall be dark-coloured, either naturally or by being stained, not painted, in such a way as not to alter the frictional characteristics of the surface. The part of the blade nearest the handle and gripped by the fingers may be covered with any material for convenience of grip, and is to be regarded as part of the handle. A side of the blade not used for striking the ball may be painted or covered with any material provided that the surface is uniformly dark-coloured and matt. A stroke with a surface other than those specified above would, however, be illegal and result in the loss of a point. Minor variations of shade, due to wear or ageing of the surface, should not be regarded as infringing the requirement for uniformity, which is intended to prevent the use of basically different colours on a single side of the bat.

Before using a racket for the first time in a match, a player shall, if so requested, show both sides of the blade to his opponent.

## 5. *The Order of Play*

In singles, the server shall first make a good service, the receiver shall then make a good return and thereafter server and receiver shall each alternately make a good return.

In doubles, the server shall first make a good service, the receiver shall then make a good return, the partner of the server shall then make a good return, the partner of the receiver shall then make a good return, and thereafter each player alternately in that sequence shall make a good return.

## 6. *A Good Service*

The ball shall be placed on the palm of the free hand, which must be stationary, open and flat, with the fingers together and the thumb free. The free hand, while in contact with the ball in service, shall at all times be above the level of the playing surface.

Service shall then begin by the server projecting the ball by hand only, without imparting spin, near vertically upwards, so that the ball be visible at all times to the umpire and so that it visibly leave the palm.

As the ball is then descending from the height of its trajectory, it shall be struck so that it touch first the server's court and then passing directly over or around the net, touch the receiver's court.

In doubles, the ball shall touch first the server's right

half-court or the centre-line on his side of the net and then, passing over or around the net, touch the receiver's right half-court or the centre-line on his side of the net.

At the moment of the impact of the racket on the ball in service, the ball shall be behind the end-line of the server's court or an imaginary extension thereof.

Strict observance of the prescribed method of service may be waived where the umpire is notified, before play begins, that compliance is prevented by physical disability.

## 7. *A Good Return*

The ball having been served or returned in play shall be struck so that it pass directly over or around the net and touch directly the opponent's court, provided that if the ball, having been served or returned in play, return with its own impetus over or around the net it may be struck while still in play so that it touch directly the opponent's court. If the ball, in passing over or around the net, touch it or its supports it shall be considered to have passed directly.

## 8. *In Play*

The ball is in play from the moment at which it is projected from the hand in service until:

- (*a*) it has touched one court twice consecutively;
- (*b*) it has, except in service, touched each court alternately without having been struck with the racket intermediately;
- (*c*) it has been struck by a player more than once consecutively;
- (*d*) it has touched a player or anything he wears or carries;
- (*e*) it has been volleyed;
- (*f*) it has touched any object other than the net, supports, or those referred to above;

(g) it has, in a doubles service, touched the left half-court of the server or of the receiver;

(h) it has, in doubles, been struck by a player out of proper sequence, except as provided in Law 15;

(i) it has, under the Expedite System, been returned by 13 successive good returns of the receiving player or pair.

## 9. *A Let*
The rally is a let:

(a) if the ball is served, in passing over the net, touch it or its supports, provided the service be otherwise good or be volleyed by the receiver;

(b) if a service be delivered when the receiver or his partner is not ready, provided always that a player may not be deemed to be unready if he or his partner attempt to strike at the ball;

(c) if, owing to an accident not within his control, a player fail to make a good service or a good return, or otherwise terminate the rally;

(d) if it be interrupted for correction of a mistake in playing order or ends;

(e) if it be interrupted for application of the Expedite System.

## 10. *A Point*
Except as provided in Law 9, a player shall lose a point:

(a) if he fail to make a good service;

(b) if a good service or a good return having been made by his opponent, he fail to make a good return;

(c) if he, or his racket, or anything that he wears or carries, touch the net or its supports while the ball is in play;

(d) if he, or his racket, or anything he wears or carries, move the playing surface while the ball is in play;

(e) if his free hand touch the playing surface while the
    ball is in play;

(f) if, before the ball in play shall have passed over the
    end-lines or side-lines not yet having touched the
    playing surface on his side of the net since being
    struck by his opponent, it come in contact with him
    or with anything he wears or carries;

(g) if he volley the ball;

(h) if, in doubles, he strike the ball out of proper
    sequence, except as provided in Law 15;

(i) if, under the Expedite System, his service and the
    twelve following strokes of the serving player or pair
    be returned by good returns of the receiving player
    or pair.

## 11. *A Game*

A game shall be won by the player or pair first scoring 21
points, unless both players or pairs shall have scored 20
points, when the winner of the game shall be the player or
pair first scoring two points more than the opposing player
or pair.

## 12. *A Match*

A match shall consist of one game, the best of three, or the
best of five games. Play shall be continuous throughout,
except that any player is entitled to claim a rest period of
not more than five minutes' duration between the third and
fourth games of a match and of not more than one minute
duration between any other successive games of a match.

## 13. *The Choice of Ends and Service*

The choice of ends and the right to serve or receive first
in a match shall be decided by toss, provided that, if the
winner of the toss choose the right to serve or receive
first, the loser shall have the choice of ends and vice versa,

and provided that the winner of the toss may, if he prefers it, require the loser to make first choice.

In doubles, the pair who have the right to serve the first five services in any game shall decide which partner shall do so. In the first game of a match the opposing pair shall then decide similarly which shall be the first receiver. In subsequent games the serving pair shall choose their first server and the first receiver will then be established automatically to correspond with the first server provided in Law 14.

## 14. *The Change of Ends and Service*

The player or pair who started at one end in a game shall start at the other in the immediately subsequent game and so on, until the end of the match. In the last possible game of the match the players or pairs shall change ends when first either player or pair reaches the score 10. In singles, after five points, the receiver shall become the server and the server the receiver, and so on until the end of the game, except as provided below. In doubles, the first five services shall be delivered by the selected partner of the pair who have the right to do so and shall be received by the appropriate partner of the opposing pair. The second five services shall be delivered by the receiver of the first five services and received by the partner of the first server. The third five services shall be delivered by the partner of the first server and received by the partner of the first receiver. The fourth five services shall be delivered by the partner of the first receiver and received by the first server. The fifth five services shall be delivered as the first five and so on, in sequence, until the end of the game except as provided below.

From the score 20-all, or if the game is being played under the Expedite System, the sequence of serving and receiving shall be the same but each player shall deliver

108

only one service in turn until the end of the game. The player or pair who served first in a game shall receive first in the immediately subsequent game.

In the last possible game of a doubles match the receiving pair shall alter its order of receiving when first either pair reaches the score 10. In each game of a doubles match the initial order of receiving shall be opposite to that in the preceding game.

### 15. *Out of Order of Ends, Serving or Receiving*

If the players have not changed ends when ends should have been changed, they shall change ends as soon as the mistake is discovered, unless a game has been completed since the error, when the error shall be ignored. In any circumstances, all points scored, before the discovery shall be reckoned.

If by mistake a player serve or receive out of his turn, play shall be interrupted as soon as the mistake is discovered and shall continue with that player serving or receiving who, according to the sequence established at the beginning of the match or at the score 10 if that sequence has been changed as provided in Law 14, should be server or receiver respectively at the score that has been reached. In any circumstances, all points scored before the discovery shall be reckoned.

### 16. *Expedite System*

If a game be unfinished 15 minutes after it has begun, the rest of that game and the remaining games of the match shall proceed under the Expedite System. Thereafter, each player shall serve one service in turn and, if the service and twelve following strokes of the serving player or pair be returned by good returns of the receiving player or pair, the server shall lose the point.

## 17. *Definitions and Interpretations*

(*a*) The period during which the ball is in play shall be termed a 'rally'. A rally the result of which is not scored shall be termed a 'let', and a rally the result of which is scored shall be termed a 'point'.

(*b*) The player who first strikes the ball during a rally shall be termed the 'server', and the player who next strikes the ball shall be termed the 'receiver'.

(*c*) The 'racket hand' is the hand carrying the racket and the 'free hand' is the hand not carrying the racket.

(*d*) 'Struck' means 'hit with the racket, carried in the racket hand, or with the racket hand below the wrist'. A stroke made with the hand alone, after dropping the racket, or by the racket after it has slipped or been thrown from the hand, is 'not good'.

(*e*) If the ball in play comes into contact with the racket or the racket hand below the wrist, not yet having touched the playing surface on one side of the net since last being struck on the other side, it shall be said to have been 'volleyed'.

(*f*) The 'playing surface' shall be regarded as including the top edges of the table, and a ball in play which strikes these latter is, therefore 'good' and still in play; if it strikes the side of the table-top below the edge it becomes out of play and counts against the last striker.

(*g*) 'Around the net' means under or around the projection of the net and its supports outside the table, but not between the end of the net and the post.

(*h*) If a player, in attempting to serve, misses the ball altogether he loses a point, because the ball is in play from the moment it is deliberately projected from the hand.